Strangers, Neighbors, Friends

Strangers, Neighbors, Friends

Muslim-Christian-Jewish Reflections
on Compassion and Peace

by

Kelly James Clark
Aziz Abu Sarah
Nancy Fuchs Kreimer

CASCADE *Books* · Eugene, Oregon

STRANGERS, NEIGHBORS, FRIENDS
Muslim-Christian-Jewish Reflections on Compassion and Peace

Cascade Books
An Imprint of Wipf and Stock Publishers
199 W. 8th Ave., Suite 3
Eugene, OR 97401

www.wipfandstock.com

PAPERBACK ISBN: 978-1-5326-1966-3
HARDCOVER ISBN: 978-1-4982-4613-2
EBOOK ISBN: 978-1-4982-4612-5

Cataloguing-in-Publication data:

Names: Clark, Kelly James, author. | Sarah, Aziz Abu, author. | Kreimer, Nancy Fuchs,
    author.
Title: Strangers, neighbors, friends : Muslim-Christian-Jewish reflections on compassion
    and peace / Kelly James Clark, Aziz Abu Sarah, and Nancy Fuchs Kreimer.
Description: Eugene, OR: Cascade Books, 2018 | Includes bibliographical references.
Identifiers: ISBN 978-1-5326-1966-3 (paperback) | ISBN 978-1-4982-4613-2 (hardcover) |
    ISBN 978-1-4982-4612-5 (ebook)
Subjects: LCSH: Religions—Relations. | Interfaith relations.
Classification: BR127 .S40 2018 (paperback) | BR127 (ebook)

Manufactured in the U.S.A.   08/03/18

To Steve Ruis, Scott Davison, and Doug Kindschi. Friends.
—KJC

To my Jewish, Christian, and Muslim teachers.
—NFK

To all my mentors and teachers
who challenged me to step out of my comfort zone
and inspired me to pursue peace and justice.
—AAS

go my friend
bestow your love
even on your enemies
if you touch their hearts
what do you think will happen

—Rumi

When will you ever, Peace, wild wooddove, shy wings shut,
Your round me roaming end, and under be my boughs?
When, when, Peace, will you, Peace?

—Gerard Manley Hopkins

"If a poetry of peace is ever to be written, there must first be this stage
we are just entering—the poetry of *preparation* for peace, a poetry
of protest, of lament, of praise for the living earth; a poetry that
demands justice, renounces violence, reveres mystery."

—Denise Levertov

Contents

Permissions

Permission to reprint copyrighted material is gratefully acknowledged to the following:

Mohja Kahf, excerpts from "All Good" from *Hagar Poems*. Copyright © 2016 by The University of Arkansas Press. Reprinted with the permission of The Permissions Company, Inc., on behalf of the publishers, www.uapress.com.

List of Contributors

Aziz Abu Sarah is an entrepreneur, speaker, peace builder, and author. He is the recipient of the Goldberg Prize for Peace in the Middle East, the Eisenhower Medallion, and the Eliav-Sartawi Award.

Kelly James Clark is Senior Research Fellow at the Kaufman Interfaith Institute at Grand Valley State University in Grand Rapids, Michigan. He is the author, editor, or coauthor of more than twenty-five books, including *Abraham's Children: Liberty and Tolerance in an Age of Religious Conflict* and *Religion and the Sciences of Origins*.

Rabbi Nancy Fuchs Kreimer is Associate Professor of Religious Studies and the founding Director of the Department of Multifaith Studies and Initiatives at the Reconstructionist Rabbinical College, where she was ordained in 1982. She coedited *Chapters of the Heart: Jewish Women Sharing the Torah of Our Lives* (Wipf and Stock, 2013).

Acknowledgments

We are grateful to Susan Matheson for her good work at every stage of writing. Kelly is grateful to Cody, Hannah, Luke, Zoe, and Rebekah at the Ferris Coffee Shop for making their shop more like a home office (but with better service).

Introduction

Kelly James Clark

Introduction

As I write, Jews and Christians in a Texas town have joined their Muslim brothers and sisters to rebuild their mosque after arson; they are contributing dollars and time to ensure them a safe place of worship. A few days earlier, an Egyptian Muslim wrapped his arms around a suicide bomber, preventing the deaths of countless Coptic Christians in Cairo at the cost of his own. Thousands upon thousands of Muslim leaders are diligently working to prevent the radicalization of individuals and to preserve peace. Jews in Israel are laying their bodies down in front of bulldozers to prevent the building of illegal settlements in the West Bank. And Christians in Canada are opening their homes and lives to Syrian refugees escaping the worst humanitarian tragedy since World War II.

You have to work really hard to hear this good news of faithful Muslims, Christians, and Jews showing compassion to those of other faiths. It's not so hard to hear of the omnipresent atrocities of ISIS and al Qaeda. Given that most Muslims, Christians, and Jews want to live in peace and bequeath better lives to their children, there is surely more good news than bad. But bad news sells. And fear drives us to atch more bad news. So the media focus on the bad, generating more prejudice and advertising revenue.

Compassion should rule in the Abrahamic religions. In each of them, compassion towards the stranger is strictly commanded. The Jewish Scriptures say: "When a stranger lives with you in your land, do not ill-treat him. The stranger who lives with you shall be treated like the native-born. Love him as yourself, for you were strangers in the land of Egypt" (Lev 19:33). Likewise, Jesus, identifying himself with needy people, said: "I was hungry and you gave me something to eat, I was thirsty and you gave me something to drink, I was a stranger and you invited me in" (Matt 25:35). And in the Quran we read: "Worship Allah and associate nothing with Him, and to parents do good, and to relatives, orphans, the needy, the near neighbor, the neighbor farther away, the companion at your side, the traveler" (Quran 4:36).

Fear, not compassion, seems to be ruling the day, driving the three Abrahamic religions apart. From the United States' drone warfare in Afghanistan and Yemen, to Israel's defiant building of settlements in the West Bank, to ISIS's vicious suicide bombings (killing mostly fellow Muslims), we are increasingly more likely to fear, ignore, dehumanize, and even harm the Abrahamic stranger than we are to invite them in. But we, Muslim-Christian-Jew alike, do so in violation of our religions' most profound understandings.

With this book, authored by three different children of Abraham, we hope to persuade Abraham's children that Christianity and Islam and Judaism, at their very best, demand compassion and kindness for strangers, sharing and suffering with neighbors, and a radically inclusive and ever-expanding circle of friends. Indeed, each religion suggests that generous and unexpected compassion, even toward the stranger, has the radical power to transform strangers into neighbors and friends. That is, Judaism, Christianity, and Islam have the spiritual and moral resources for Muslims, Christians, and Jews to get along, to live together in mutual peace and harmony.

In this book we'll focus on how, without loss of genuine faith, Christians, Muslims, and Jews can and should overcome their fears and cultivate and work for peace, liberty, and compassion

I enlisted Nancy Fuchs Kreimer and Aziz Abu Sarah to join me in writing from our own faith perspectives. Our aim is to inform and inspire faith-based action—to courageously extend our divinely motivated love beyond family, friend, and neighbor to the stranger.

Before concluding the introduction, listen to Nancy and Aziz in their own voices.

Nancy Fuchs Kreimer

I am an associate professor of religious studies and the founding director of the Department of Multifaith Studies and Initiatives at the Reconstructionist Rabbinical College in Wyncote, Pennsylvania, just north of Philadelphia. I was ordained at the Reconstructionist Rabbinical College in 1982. I also hold a master's degree from Yale Divinity School and a doctorate from Temple University. I have developed community-based learning opportunities for rabbinical students and their Christian and Muslim peers. I am a founding member of the Interfaith Center of Philadelphia, Shoulder-to-Shoulder of the Islamic Society of North America, and the Sisterhood of Salaam Shalom. I recently coedited *Chapters of the Heart: Jewish Women Sharing the Torah of our Lives* (Wipf and Stock, 2013), which was a finalist for a 2014 National Jewish Book Award.

When my daughter was little, someone asked her if her father practiced law. "Practiced?" she exclaimed. "He doesn't have to practice! He knows!" Well, he was, indeed, a knowledgeable lawyer, but he also had to practice. After all these years, I am still "practicing" Judaism. That means, first and foremost, becoming what we call in Yiddish, a *mensch*. It is the work of a lifetime.

Much of what I know about the practice of Judaism will be in the Torah and rabbinic writings—but not all. Some is from the wisdom of the Yiddish language, a pastiche of German and Hebrew that encodes life lessons in its very vocabulary, but so much more. Some of what I know about the practice of Judaism comes from medieval Hebrew poetry; from contemporary Jewish theologians, novelists, and psychologists; from true tales of the Holocaust or of modern Israel; and from the life stories of Jewish men and women who have inspired me. I have also learned much from the privilege I have had, as a Jew, of encountering and working with men and women of other faiths who are working equally hard to practice their own.

Encountering other faiths has, in the end, changed me and my Judaism. For me, the theological work, the political work, and the personal work have all been a religious practice. In this book, I hope to show how this practice emerges from and is sustained by my reading of Jewish tradition.

You might be wondering: What is that "reading" she is talking about? Is she uncovering the true "essence of Judaism" or inventing a new Judaism in keeping with her own values and vision? Let me tell you why I think there is a better question to ask.

Jews have always been inventing Judaism. I do not believe Judaism is "all about peace" any more than I think it is "all about violence." I know from my study of Jewish thought over thousands of years that we have both peace and violence in our texts. I trust my tradition enough not to fear that messiness. Not only has Judaism evolved over the centuries; we are currently in a time of very rapid change. As a rabbi, I believe it is my responsibility to uncover the teachings that will help us move forward in this globalizing world. So the better question to ask is: How can we lift up those teachings that are most generative of peace and compassion for our time and place?

Aziz Abu Sarah

I am, first and foremost, a Palestinian from Jerusalem. I am many other things—a National Geographic Explorer and Cultural Educator, a TED Fellow, a businessman, a peace worker—but I am, again most fundamentally, a Jerusalemite Palestinian. Nothing has shaped me more than growing up in Israel and the West Bank during successive intifadas as an outsider Palestinian. Although my experiences radicalized me as a young man, I found my way to peace and justice. You'll need to read my chapters to find out why and how. I seek in all that I do the intersection of my vocation and social justice.

I am the cofounder of MEJDI Tours, a social enterprise focused on introducing multi-narrative cultural expeditions to the travel industry. MEJDI has been recognized by the United Nations World Tourism Organization and the United Nations Alliance of Civilizations for its innovations in travel and education.

I also served as the executive director of the Center for World Religions, Diplomacy, and Conflict Resolution at George Mason University (2009–2015) and was chairman of the Bereaved Families Forum, a joint Israeli-Palestinian reconciliation organization (2006–2010). I have pioneered and managed projects in conflict resolution and community relations in Afghanistan, Iran, Syria, Turkey, Jordan, and the United States. I recently cofounded the "I Am Your Protector" interfaith campaign and "Project Amal ou Salam," a grassroots relief and educational organization for Syrian refugees in Turkey, Jordan, Syria, and Lebanon. I coproduced the National Geographic web series "Conflict Zone," which explores the Israeli-Palestinian conflict from the perspective of Palestinian refugees, the Israeli Defense Forces, and Jewish settlers.

I have been honored to receive numerous awards, including the Goldberg Prize for Peace in the Middle East from the Institute of International Education and the Eliav-Sartawi Award for Middle Eastern Journalism from Search for Common Ground. United Nations Secretary-General Ban Ki-moon recognized my work during his speech at the 5th Global Forum of the UN Alliance of Civilizations in February 2013, and I have been named one of the "500 Most Influential Muslims" by the Royal Islamic Strategic Studies Centre for the past six years.

But I am, at bottom, a Palestinian seeking and working for peace.

Kelly James Clark

I began writing academic articles on tolerance in the mid-1990s at the instigation of my good Jewish friend, Stewart Shapiro. Stewart and I spent the year together on sabbatical at St. Andrews University in Scotland. On our regular walks, he pressed me to reconsider Christianity's treatment of Jews and asked if Christianity could undergird genuine tolerance of other religions. So I wrote a series of scholarly articles that analyzed the concept of tolerance, which were read by probably a half-dozen people.

As I approached age fifty, I was growing increasingly aware of the irrelevance of most abstract, academic philosophy and increasingly concerned about events in the world. So I shifted my focus to speaking more directly to issues involving religion and tolerance. To that end, I commissioned essays from fifteen prominent Muslims, Christians, and Jews—including former President Jimmy Carter and Abdurrahman Wahid, the first democratically elected president of Indonesia—to address liberty and tolerance from their own faith perspectives. This resulted in the publication of *Abraham's Children: Liberty and Tolerance in An Age of Religious Conflict* (Yale University Press, 2012) and a conference in Washington, DC on the tenth anniversary of 9/11.

I am often criticized for defending tolerance. "People," my critics say, "don't want to be merely tolerated, they want to be accepted and loved." But my response is that they need to talk to more people. People who are being killed or imprisoned or denied other basic human rights because of their religious beliefs *do* want their beliefs and practices to be tolerated. If their societies could move from persecution to toleration, their lives would be vastly better. Would that we were at the stage of human history where we could go beyond tolerance.

Moreover, I do *not* think that we tolerate (put up with, endure) people. We should tolerate beliefs and behaviors but never people—we should and must respect every human being. Indeed, our respect for other people grounds principled tolerance, that is, it motivates our willingness to allow them to choose their own deepest beliefs and practices (even if we strongly disagree with those beliefs and practices). I think it a lack of respect for other humans, which results in our dehumanizing those who are different from ourselves, that lies at the root of intolerance and violence.

I aim, then, in my chapters, to show that Christianity, best and most deeply understood, demands respect for and even love of stranger. More deeply, it calls Christians to love others as they love themselves and even more radically, to love their enemies.

Conclusion

I stand on the beach and watch the rushing water seek out all the low places, its wriggling fingers reaching out to find and fill empty space. Its reach exhausted, another wave follows and fills those empty places. And another. There are always more; more than enough. Abundance. I want to extend my arms in grace and mercy to find and fill the world's empty spaces. When compassion and joy fill in the holes, the cracks and crevices, the nooks and crannies and hidden places, peace and harmony overflow with the rightness of the world.

Aziz Abu Sarah

1

Life and Death

It was a typical cold January day in 1988, and I was bored as usual. As a rambunctious seven-year-old and the youngest of my six siblings, I usually finished school around noon and then headed home. I lived in Bethany, a small Palestinian village just outside of Jerusalem. Although I was oblivious then, I'm not now: Bethany was dismal. It had no community centers, public parks, or playgrounds—just rocky hills, dusty shops, and crumbling streets.

I joined up with other kids from the neighborhood and, as we often did, we milled around in the street. One of the kids had an idea. He thought we should do what we had all seen older Palestinian students doing on television: throw rocks. A solution to our boredom! I thought we should do it, too. We headed to the nearest road, and for the next hour, we exuberantly hurled stones at the passing vehicles. While most of our stones fell short of their mark, one or two eventually connected with their targets. A car swerved to a stop and its angry driver jumped out shaking his fist and chasing us. We scattered and scrambled back to our homes, partly scared, partly exhilarated.

Later that evening, my furious parents dragged me out of my room, livid at having learned from a neighbor (whose car we had hit) of my new hobby. I was confused. As a seven-year-old, I couldn't understand what the big deal was. After all, older and wiser Palestinian kids threw small rocks at big cars. What's the harm?

As my parents persisted, I eventually concluded where we had gone wrong: we threw rocks at our neighbors. We should have thrown rocks at *Israeli* cars—*not* our neighbors' cars because they know where we live and they spoke to our families!

This how I first came to understand that I was living in a conflict zone in which our community (the Palestinians) was locked in a struggle with the Israelis. My awareness of the conflict grew as the battles drew nearer, the weapons grew bigger, and the consequences were more severe.

My friends and I located a strategic road with Israeli cars; one where we could easily hide and quickly escape. One day, we hit the window of a bus with a rock. We were so excited by our conquest that we started arguing about whose stone had connected. While we were debating, a man jumped out of the bus and aimed a rifle at us. When two loud shots rang out, we ran, terrified. That was the first time I had been shot at. I was eight years old.

In spite of my very real fears, I was emboldened by the confidence of youth. I thought I was invincible.

Each year during Ramadan, my dad would wake us before sunrise to drink water and eat before the start of the day's fast. One morning, my dad woke us up around four o'clock. My brothers and I were tired and grumpy. After eating and drinking, we shuffled back to bed. I was nine and shared a twin bed with my older brother, Tayseer, who was eighteen. It was late spring, and the birds were starting to sing as the sky turned from black to navy blue to sky blue.

I was dozing off when I heard loud shouting and a heavy pounding on the front door. Our bedroom door crashed open, and a group of Israeli soldiers brandishing machine guns barged into our room. They ordered us to our feet and demanded our identity cards. I quaked in fear as my four older brothers handed over their documents. The soldiers never asked for mine. They examined my brothers' cards, held a clipped conversation in Hebrew, and then grabbed Tayseer and dragged him out. My mom cried and begged, pleading with the officer not to hurt him. She had heard about the Israeli military torturing Palestinian prisoners. The Israelis called it their "break the bones" policy. The officer promised that he would take Tayseer and just "ask him a few questions."

This Ramadan was no celebration; it was one of the longest months of our lives. We were depressed, anxious, and helpless. We didn't find out where Tayseer was being held for more than two weeks. The Red Cross eventually arranged for my dad to visit him. Dad returned from his visit visibly shaken. Although Tayseer's mouth was bloodied, my brother said only that his tooth was hurting him. A few weeks later, I visited him. The journey to the prison took a full day of passing through dehumanizing checkpoints where we waited in long lines and were harassed by border guards. Once at the prison, I stared at my brother through the two fences that separated us. The visit lasted only a few minutes. I was barely able to say hello.

He was released from prison about eight months later. His body was badly beaten, the result of repeated torture. They didn't just ask him a few questions; they employed their hideous "break their bones" policy on my brother. We rushed Tayseer directly to the hospital, but he had massive internal bleeding and liver and spleen failure. There was nothing the surgeons could do to save him. He died after coming out of surgery. My nineteen-year-old brother, Tayseer, was tortured to death in an Israeli prison for being suspected of throwing rocks at military jeeps.

Tayseer's death enraged me. I was consumed by loss, emptiness, and fury. I spent the rest of my childhood feeling that I had a duty to him, to avenge his murder and fight back against Israeli oppression. I was determined to avenge my brother's death.

By the time I was thirteen, I had become politically active. I constantly read the news and participated in protests that sometimes turned violent. When I turned sixteen, I became a leader in the youth movement for Fatah, one of the largest Palestinian political parties. I became an editor for a Fatah youth magazine in Jerusalem, writing pamphlets and mobilizing new members.

Growing up as a Palestinian in Jerusalem meant living in constant insecurity. We lived in Bethany, about three miles east of the center of East Jerusalem, in a house my father had built. The Israeli government decided that area was outside the border of the municipality of East Jerusalem, and because we could not prove that we lived within the Jerusalem municipality borders, we had difficulty passing through checkpoints into Jerusalem. Legally, I could no longer attend my school in Jerusalem, but for months I continued to attend illegally, sneaking around checkpoints, facing beatings when I got caught and being fired at when I was too far away for the soldiers to run after me.

Before I left for school each morning, my mom would pack me an onion. Schoolbooks, homework, pencils, and lunch were secondary to the onion because we believed an onion would protect us against tear gas.

Eventually, when I was sixteen, we abandoned our precious home in Bethany because my family was stripped of their rights and benefits, such as social security and health insurance. We left the spacious, six-bedroom home and were forced into a small, stuffy, two-bedroom rental apartment in Jerusalem, which housed me, my parents, my three brothers, two sisters-in-law, and four nieces and nephews. It took us a few months to find a larger apartment in Jerusalem.

The dismal life of a Palestinian boy—displaced, disenfranchised, and distressed—is fertile ground for the radicalization of justifiably angry young men.

While it is often appropriate to punish wicked deeds, my parents repeatedly reminded me of the higher and more beautiful path, the path of forgiveness (Quran 42:40). They were constantly worried that I would seek revenge and end up being killed. They encouraged me to avoid politics. Believers are repeatedly encouraged to be forgiving and compassionate people who, according to the Quran, "control their rage and pardon other people" (3:134). My parents would say this repeatedly, but I was not yet in a position to hear.

2

Crossing Enemy Lines

———

It was my first day in *ulpan*, a school where Jewish newcomers to Israel go to learn Hebrew, the language I had resented for years. It was, after all, the language of the "enemy." How could I learn the language of those who killed my brother? But I had to face the reality that living in Jerusalem without being fluent in Hebrew would be detrimental to my future. I would not be able to get a decent job, study at a decent university, or have a promising career without it. Hebrew, dammit, was a must.

I was eighteen years old and had just finished high school. I had never had a Jewish friend; I had never even had a normal conversation with a Jewish person. As a Palestinian growing up in Jerusalem, I lived in a Palestinian neighborhood, went to Palestinian schools, read Palestinian textbooks, shopped in Palestinian markets, watched Palestinian television shows, and took Palestinian taxis. Although I had held a few small jobs washing dishes and cleaning floors in Israeli venues, I never had a conversation with a Jew. For the previous eighteen years I saw Israelis and Jews (to me they were the same) as enemies.

My only interactions with Israelis had been at checkpoints. While Israelis can speed by checkpoints, Palestinians are forced to wait in long lines, often for hours and in oppressive heat, and are often intimidated, harassed, or humiliated by the Israeli Defense Forces before being allowed to pass. I had to wait in these lines every day just to get to school. Palestinians and women in labor have died waiting in these wretched lines while trying to get to a hospital. In a famous video of a checkpoint, an Israeli border guard can be heard saying, "Animals. Animals. Like the Discovery Channel. All of Ramallah is a jungle. There are monkeys, dogs, gorillas. The problem is that the animals are locked, they can't come out. We're humans. They're animals. They aren't humans, we are."[1] As you might expect, some of my interactions were terrible and included detentions and beatings. Most of the guards were nice. Some would even joke with us. However, you can't really have a meaningful dialogue with someone holding a gun!

Now that I was "forced" to learn Hebrew, I was determined simply to learn the language, not make friends. I walked into the class and quickly saw that I was the only Palestinian. There were a few non-Jews—Christians but no other Palestinians or Muslims—but the majority were Jewish. I sat down quickly, closed myself within, and was determined not to talk. I was in the enemy's lair and I was scared to death. My heart pounded faster and faster. I felt that everyone was looking at me, judging me, hating me. Surely they were thinking, "Why is this Arab here?" They probably also saw me as an enemy; maybe they were afraid. I was scared, uncomfortable, and frustrated. I wanted to run out of the door. In this foreign situation, surrounded by the enemy, I didn't know how to act.

When the teacher approached me and said, "Hi, how are you" in Arabic, I was confused. And then even more so when she smiled and warmly welcomed me to the class. This was the very first time I'd been recognized as a human being by an Israeli.

My fellow students went out of their way to include me in their conversations, not only to help me learn Hebrew but also to learn about me and my life. The teacher broke us up into small groups and we would have to ask each other simple questions: "What is your name?" and "Where are you from?" and "What do you eat?" As I found myself thinking that these are nice people, I also found myself wondering how that was possible; I was slowly overwhelmed by their kindness. Against every fiber of my being and against my explicit intentions, I had a change of heart.

I remember learning that some of my fellow students liked country music, like me, and that we shared a special appreciation for Johnny Cash. Most of my Palestinian friends could care less about Johnny Cash. They were into pop music. I soon felt comfortable making jokes and fooling around with the same people I wouldn't have even considered saying "hi" to

1. "Checkpoints 101," *Occupied Palestine.*

8

a few weeks ago. I argued about the Israeli love of instant coffee versus the Palestinian love of Arabic cardamom-flavored brewed coffee. (I was right, of course, and they were wrong.)

From country music to coffee, we had become friends.

But life isn't all country music and coffee. Eventually, we had to talk about the elephant in the room—politics. It started when my teacher talked about David Ben-Gurion, the founding father of the State of Israel and its first prime minister. Ben-Gurion led Israel's 1948 Arab-Israeli war, when 700,000 Palestinian Arabs were expelled or fled from the area that became Israel. He is not held in high regard by Palestinians, to say the least.

My teacher suddenly looked at me and said, "For Palestinians, Yasser Arafat is their Ben-Gurion. He is the founder of their state." I was astonished to hear an Israeli Jew say something positive about Arafat, the leader of the Palestinian Liberation Organization (PLO) and the Palestinian Authority at that time. As leader of the PLO, which was considered by Israelis an anti-Israel terrorist organization, Arafat was not held in high regard by the Israelis. Then she lowered her voice and said, "Some Israelis would throw me out of this window if they heard me say anything good about Yasser Arafat."

In subsequent discussions, I learned that many Israelis opposed the occupation of the Palestinian territories and Israel's military rule over millions of Palestinians. I had no idea there were Jews who were sympathetic to the plight of my people. Many Israelis (and some Israeli organizations) saw me not as a demographic threat, an enemy, or a backward Arab; instead, they saw me as a human being and a friend.

I slowly realized that I would have to rethink my beliefs and ideology. I had been full of rage and anger for years. Had I wrongly demonized all Israelis due to the actions of their government and their military? But the harder question for me was: had I been a slave to a life chosen for me by the murderers of my brother? I came to realize that my brother's killers had been destroying my life, too.

I began to think: *I have to take charge of my own life and make my own decisions, regardless of what others do. I can't let those who murdered Tayseer drown me in my hatred and anger. I can choose to respond with hatred and violence, or with grace and love.*

As I listened to others, I realized that I knew nothing of the Israeli narrative, including the Holocaust. When asked about the Holocaust, I always felt the defensive urge to say, "Hey, it wasn't my fault! Heck, given Israeli occupation, I've suffered from it, too." I felt that if I were to acknowledge Israel's suffering, I would betray my own people's suffering. Some part of me feared that if I sympathized with "the enemy," I'd lose my right to fight for justice.

And yet this kind of transforming empathy was valued by the Prophet who wrote, "Grievous to him is what you suffer" (Quran 9:128). His empathetic response to those who suffered was kindness and mercy. I have since discovered that you are stronger when you let empathy overcome enmity. That lesson, however, was a hard one to learn.

I decided that Yad Vashem, a museum and Israel's official memorial to the victims of the Holocaust, would be the best place to start understanding the Israeli perspective. As I crossed the threshold of Yad Vashem, my heart was racing; I was keenly aware that I was the only Palestinian in the entire museum. As I looked at the pictures and read the stories, however, my self-consciousness was replaced with shock. I could not believe that human beings could become so denigrated they could commit such atrocities against fellow human beings.

After sympathetically hearing the Israeli story, which began at the Holocaust museum, I chose grace and love. Choosing to respond with love was transformational for me. First and foremost, I decided to forgive. I forgave, not because the person who killed my brother deserved it (or had asked for it), but because I wanted to be the kind of person who forgives. Regardless of the murderer's contrition (or lack of it), I would be a forgiver.

Here is one concrete change in me. When a bomb goes off in West Jerusalem, I don't think (as I did before), "They are my enemy, who cares?" I have started to think, "Wait, my friends live there," and I call to make sure my friends are safe. My Israeli friends do the same for me.

My journey to forgiveness began with my willingness to step out of my comfort zone and into an uncomfortable zone. I felt I needed to learn more about Judaism, so, as a college student, I worked in an ultra-Orthodox neighborhood. I also felt I needed to learn more about Christianity, so I attended an evangelical Bible college in Jerusalem. Initially, I was always the "other," but we then ended up becoming friends.

Years later, I worked on a National Geographic web series about the Israeli-Palestinian conflict, and when we were filming and interviewing the Israeli army, I sometimes experienced pain when I recalled vivid memories of my brother. But I was also challenged in my comfortable assumptions about the "enemy." The Israeli-Palestinian conflict, I have come to learn, is complicated, and both sides have blood on their hands. But fighting for justice or the end of occupation no longer meant that I must hate. These experiences slowly transformed me, giving me a much better understanding of—and compassion for—others.

From Hebrew school to the Holocaust museum, I learned to choose compassion. "Grievous to me is what you suffer." Choosing love crowded out all thoughts of revenge, and I began to act with kindness and mercy.

3

Fighting Fear

Our little plane bounced in the wind as we flew over the mountains on our way to Afghanistan. It was just the beginning of a journey in which we all had to face new fears; flying in a floppy plane over mountains would be the least of them. I was headed to Kabul with my colleagues from George Mason University for a project that would create a Muslim leadership network to counter the jihadi Taliban recruitment of new members. We hoped this new network would help shape a peaceful future for Afghanistan, even though, only months before, a wave of suicide bombings and attacks on government buildings, hotels, and shopping centers had shaken Kabul. Some of those bombings were just a few blocks from where we were meeting. Our hotel itself was bombed before (and after) our stay.

Once we landed in Kabul, we took a van to a government building for our meeting. In a war zone, the entryway of a building is the most dangerous place to be because suicide bombers prevented from entering often detonate just outside the door. So when you're waiting outside a government building in Afghanistan, your heart beats rapidly and your mind plays tricks on you. With every passing car, you imagine a burst of light or a Kalashnikov rifle aimed at your head. We spent a nerve-wracking fifteen minutes standing at the checkpoint in front of the concrete structure feeling very exposed. I couldn't imagine what must go through the minds of the police officers standing outside these buildings all day every day, knowing that they might be attacked. What kept them there, willing to sacrifice their lives for those inside? Duty or desperation to make a living?

To relieve our nervousness as we waited, I cracked jokes with Scott—an American Jew, who had recently quit his job at a bank to study conflict resolution at George Mason University. In conflict resolution, we often resort to morbid humor to cope with the death and suffering around us. Scott joked that with his white face and blue eyes he felt like an obvious target for attackers.

After the longest fifteen minutes of my life, we were allowed inside and led to a large, simply decorated room. About fifteen men dressed in traditional Afghan clothes—knee-length tunics, baggy pants, turbans, and a vest or suit jacket—were sitting on the carpets in the center of the room. After shaking hands with everyone, we sat down next to former Afghan President Burhanuddin Rabbani and began to talk about the Muslim network we hoped to build.

Rabbani was a Muslim cleric and a former Afghan warlord. In the 1980s, he courageously led bands of mujahedeen in the fight against the Soviet Union. By 1992, the hardened imam had helped topple the Communist government and conquer Kabul before becoming the president of Afghanistan. He ruled for four years until 1996 when the Taliban rolled into Kabul with tanks. The Taliban captured and tortured Rabbani's predecessor, Mohammad Najibullah, and hung his body from a lamppost. Rabbani managed to escape.

Now, years later, Rabbani was leading the Afghanistan High Peace Council and serving as the chief negotiator in talks with those same Taliban fighters.

Rabbani asked us to tell something about ourselves and our backgrounds. When my turn came, I told him that I was a Palestinian from a Muslim family living in Jerusalem. As tears welled up in his eyes, he interrupted me. "I have a deep love for Palestine," he explained. "During the fight against the Soviets, one of my compatriots was a Palestinian Muslim who left Palestine to help Afghanistan. This man sacrificed his life for my country."

Without skipping a beat, he switched from Dari to classical Arabic—the Arabic of the Quran. Classical Arabic is not commonly spoken; it is reserved mainly for writing and television news programs. A warlord's mastery of it was surprising; however for a pious man, classical Arabic is important for reading the Quran. I had learned classical Arabic in my elementary Islamic schools where we had daily lessons on it. Most of the people in the room, including my partners and translators, didn't understand the Arabic we were speaking. In a room full of people, we had our own intimate conversation. He asked about the situation in my home country and described at length his love for Palestine, and told me that he hoped it would be free some day.

In our meeting, Rabbani was hopeful that he could strike a deal with the Taliban and save Afghanistan from further bloodshed. His peaceful vision was to unite all segments of Afghan society—the Taliban and the other political groups; the multiethnic communities, such as the Pashtuns, Tajiks, and Hazara; and the Shias and Sunnis. Afghanistan's immense variety of ethnic and religious groups would require a cooperative approach to peace.

I asked him what motivated his important but dangerous work and he referred to Quran 8:61: "And if they incline to peace, then incline to it [also] and rely upon Allah." He said, "If people are willing to talk about peace, then we are ordered by God to talk to them."

I was moved. I had heard stories about Rabbani's violent past fighting the Soviets, but I didn't know which stories were true and which were myths. Although the idea of meeting with a former warlord had initially made me wary, I saw that he was now committed to peace. This "warlord" understood in a deep way that obedience to Allah requires listening to anyone with even the slightest inclination toward peace.

I wanted to be part of this man's peace initiative with the Taliban. But would he agree to take me with him? After all, we had only just met, and he barely knew anything about me, except the name of my homeland. I couldn't ask in English because my partners—both the Afghans and the Americans—would forbid my participation in the negotiations. So I asked in classical Arabic if I could attend the negotiations with the Taliban representative.

Rabbani responded by quoting Quran 49:13: "O mankind, indeed We have created you from male and female and made you peoples and tribes that you may know one another." He was illustrating that Muslims must learn to live in diverse communities and that God sees differences as positive elements of the societies he created. He then said, quite simply, "Yes, of course you can come."

I was excited and honored to have the chance to work with Rabbani for peace. Still, I was nervous. What could I bring to the table? If I feared meeting one warlord, how would I do in a room full of them? Was it really safe to be in such a place?

After returning to Washington, DC, I looked forward to my next trip to Afghanistan and to the negotiations between Rabbani and the Taliban.

A few months later I received a text message from Scott: "Check the news immediately. You won't believe what happened."

I ran to my computer and read the headline: "Rabbani Dead in Suicide Attack by Taliban Negotiator." I was overwhelmed with sadness and anger. A good man—a man I respected and had grown to care for, a man who could have brought peace to a region ravaged by war—had been killed in a vicious attack.

How did a suicide bomber get into that building? In an effort to foster goodwill, the guards had only cursorily searched the Taliban negotiator; security had neglected to check his turban (in which he had concealed a bomb). Searches are sensitive issues: leaders often feel insulted if they are asked to submit to an invasive search, and the demand to go through a metal detector can be a sign of mistrust. Sometimes for sensitive meetings, I've spent more time negotiating on security and metal detectors than on major issues, like jihad and women's roles in Islam. Rabbani's bomber had already attended several meetings with the peace council; he had likely gained their trust (or at least forced them into a position where they had to act like they trusted him). Subsequent searches would have been taken as signs of both disrespect and distrust and would have adversely affected the sensitive negotiations. The desire not to offend cost Rabbani his life.

When the Taliban negotiator walked into the room, he bowed down as a sign of respect. When his turban touched Rabbani's, he detonated the explosives.

How could a person who knew Rabbani's deep desire for peace decide to kill him? Didn't his killer know that the Quran expressly forbids killing fellow Muslims? "Whoever kills a believer intentionally, his punishment is hell to live therein forever. He shall incur the wrath of Allah, Who will lay His curse on him and prepare for him a woeful punishment" (Quran 4:93).

It made me wonder if you can really negotiate with such single-minded radicals, ones with little apparent concern for life, truth, and the Quran.

The Islam I grew up with would never have considered let alone condoned blowing up a peacemaker. The stories of the Prophet Muhammad that I had learned as a child differed vastly from the violent sort of "Islam" we find in al-Qaeda, ISIS, and the Taliban. Although Islam is not a pacifist religion, the stories I grew up with consistently and enthusiastically promoted peace and forgiveness.

For example, the Prophet tells us that if you have a fight with your brother for more than three days, God will not accept your petitions and you will lose your place in the afterlife. And, through the Prophet, God commands Muslims not to hate fellow Muslims or to cut off relationships with them.[1]

I found myself perplexed: how could a faithful Muslim look at these Scriptures and hadiths and then decide that it was permissible to kill someone in his own home who was negotiating for peace?

Islam is first and foremost faith in and submission to one God, Allah. It finds its most basic and deep expressions in prayer, tithing, fasting, and worship. These so-called pillars of Islam—faith, prayer, tithing, fasting, and pilgrimage—concern the creation of a spiritual connection between a person and God. Islam revolves around things like family, neighborhood, spirituality, community, and relationships. Muslims, then, follow the Prophet away from enmity and violence and toward peace and reconciliation.

But more important than these expressions of faith is our commitment to peace. As Said ibn al-Musayyib recounted the Prophet saying, "Shall I tell you what is better than much prayer and sadaqa [giving to the needy]? Mending discord. And beware of hatred—it strips you of your religion."[2] Mending discord and fighting hatred are more important than two of the pillars of Islam. If prayer and tithing are the pillars of Islam, compassion and peace—*not* revenge and violence— are the cornerstones of Islam.

Rabbani understood that the heart of Islam is peace. His vision of peace cost him his life. The struggle against those who push for extremist versions of Islam is a struggle for the soul of the religion, and it is a defining moment for Islam. True Muslims must overcome in this struggle.

---

1. Sahih al-Bukhari Vol. 8, Book 73, Hadith 91 (Bukhari 6065).
2. ibn Anas, *Muwatta Malik*, Book 47, Hadith 7 (Malik 1642).

4

Prayer

When I was eight years old, I attended a summer camp at the Al-Aqsa mosque in Jerusalem. One day my teacher said to me, "I haven't seen you praying with the other students. Are you okay?"

We had been studying Islam and other topics to prepare us for the next academic year, so it was a perfectly appropriate question. It would have been hard not to notice my absence. Muslims pray five times a day, and we prayed as a group during the camp.

The reason I hadn't been praying with the other students was because I had come to the conclusion that I no longer needed to pray five times per day. I had been told at camp that a single prayer prayed in the Al-Aqsa mosque is worth 500 prayers prayed elsewhere. It wasn't hard, even at age eight, to do the mental math. Every prayer at the Al-Asqa mosque is the equivalent of a hundred days of daily prayers; four prayers in Al-Asqa, then, and I was done for the entire year! I had decided to pray once a month in the Al-Aqsa mosque (twelve times a year instead of the calculated four, just to be safe) and to stop worrying about daily prayers.

I said to my teacher, "I've done the calculations: I've prayed enough for this week, and I'm good for a year now!"

While my teacher gently laughed at me, he corrected me: "Prayer is not a credit system to fulfill a menial obligation. It is your daily connection with Allah, where you cleanse yourself, you remember to submit to God, and you find peace."

Prayer, one of the five pillars of Islam, is the most virtuous act for a Muslim. We read of Muhammad's followers: "The first matter that the servant will be brought to account for on the Day of Judgment is the prayer. If it is sound, then the rest of his deeds will be sound. And if it is bad, then the rest of his deeds will be bad."[1] Prayer, then, is the spiritual key.

The first surah in the Quran, *al-Fatiha* ("the key"), is recited in every prayer and is a personal prayer centering the human spirit on the will of God. With every recitation, the worshipper enters into intimate dialogue with God:

> In the name of God, Most Gracious, Most Merciful.
> Praise be to God, Lord of the universe.
> Most Gracious, Most Merciful.
> Master of the Day of Judgment.
> Only You we worship; only You we ask for help.
> Guide us in the right path;
> The path of those whom You blessed.

Before prayers, Muslims "purify themselves" through ritualistic bathing (*wudu*). Through *wudu* Muslims literally remove the grime and grease from their body, but figuratively we are removing the spiritual impurities from our hearts. *Wudu* is a reminder of good spiritual hygiene, most clearly attained through sincere prayer. We read:

> "If a person had a stream outside his door and he bathed in it five
> times a day, do you think he would have any filth left on him?"
> [asked the Prophet].
>   The people said, "No filth would remain on him whatsoever."
>   The Prophet (peace be upon him) then said, "That is like the
> five daily prayers: Allah wipes away the sins by them."[2]

Prayer, then, is a spiritual cleansing. But why five times a day? Christians and Jews don't pray five times a day. Only three prayers (*salat*) are mentioned by name in the Quran: *Salat Al-Fajr* (Dawn Prayer) 24:58; *Salat Al-Isha* (Night Prayer) 24:58; *Al-Salat Al-Wusta* (The Middle Prayer) 2:238. However, 99 percent of all Muslims in the world claim that God decreed five daily prayers. In a Hadith, Allah tells Muhammad that his followers

1. Recorded by al-Tabarani. According to Al-Albani, *Sahih al-Jami*, vol.1, p. 503.
2. Sahih al-Bukhari, Vol. 8, Book 73, Hadith 91 (Bukhari 6065).

should pray fifty times a day. When Moses reminds Muhammad that his people aren't likely to be so diligent, Muhammad petitions God and it gets knocked down to five times per day!

But whether fifty or five or three times a day, the chief purpose of prayer is the continual submission of yourself to God. In genuine prayer one brings together all of Islam (submission) in one neat package: one's faith (*imaan*), God-consciousness (*taqwa*), sincerity (*ikhlas*), and worship of Allah (`*ibaadah*). Faithfully and sincerely worshipping the one God, I am constantly reminded only Allah is God. Money is not my god, food is not my god, fame is not my god, my country is not my god. And, most importantly, I am not God. Five times a day, a Muslim humbly bows down before the only being worthy of worship, to remind his or her overweening self that they are not God.

I remember asking our neighborhood imam if I could learn how to make the call of prayer. The wizened imam with his disheveled beard smiled and said yes. For the next few days, he taught me and a couple of friends about the call of prayer. We learned to say and then to feel the deep meaning of the words, "God is Great, I testify that there is no god except GOD."

Finally, I don't see how any genuine Muslim can sincerely pray to God, with all that that implies and involves, and then assume the godlike authority to take another human being's life. To decide to take a human life is to make a decision that only God has the authority to make. To take a life, then, is to believe oneself to be God, that is, to commit idolatry of the worst sort. And the only antidote to idolatry is sincere prayer. It is even more baffling to me the amount of suicide bombings that happen in mosques by people who claim to follow God. Those who understand Islam couldn't have carried out attacks on mosques, churches, and synagogues in Jerusalem, Egypt, Saudi Arabia, and other places. No true believer in God would ever kill someone else while praying in a mosque, church, synagogue, or any other temple.

Prayer and worship is also about action. I remember my teacher telling us a story about Omar Ibn Alkhatab, the second caliph: he would not memorize more than ten verses of the Quran until he understood them and applied them. I found that the purpose of prayer in Islam, Christianity, and Judaism is similar. It is not about showing off one's piety, but rather about having a true connection with God and finding inner peace by understanding that there is a supreme God in control of all things.

5

Fasting

"Tomorrow is Ramadan," the television anchor announced. Officials had seen the new crescent moon, which signals the beginning of Ramadan. Muslims around the world cling to the tradition of the phases of the moon determining the beginning and the end of Ramadan, a Muslim holy month where fasting is observed from sunrise to sunset. Muslims fast the entire ninth month of the Muslim year to commemorate the first revelation of the Quran to Muhammad.

I recall my first fast. It was spring, and I was six years old. I was so excited about my first Ramadan fast, and so afraid! Fasting seemed hard because it meant . . . well, not eating or drinking and I, like every other six-year-old, liked to eat.

My first day was hard. I lasted until noon, but then I had to drink some water. Every day I tried a little harder. I didn't want to disappoint my mother, so for a few days I lied and said I had fasted all day. But I had snuck sips of water from the bathroom sink. Like most moms, my mom knew I was lying. She patiently reminded me that I shouldn't fast for her but for God. By the end of the month, I was able to fast the entire day. I was a proud six-year-old.

During Ramadan, Muslims abstain, from dawn to dusk, not only from food but also from beverages, smoking, and sexual relations. "Abu Huraira related that the Prophet (peace and blessings be upon him) said: 'Whoever fasts during Ramadan with faith and seeking his reward from Allah will have his past sins forgiven'" (Bukhari, Muslim). Muslims are likewise required to abstain from any sinful behavior that might negate the rewards of fasting, such as hypocrisy, lying, and fighting (abstaining from sin is more important than fasting and prayer). That is, we fast not only with our bodies but also with our hearts. We read: "Abu Huraira related that the Prophet said: 'If a person does not avoid false talk and false conduct during Siyam, then Allah does not care if he abstains from food and drink'" (Bukhari, Muslim). Through fasting and prayer, one seeks spiritual liberation from slavery to one's physical desires, devoting one's purified heart and mind more completely to God (*taqwa*). A mind set on God is a mind set on righteousness and peace.

But Ramadan is not just about a believer and his or her personal relationship with God. Ramadan unites Muslims together around the world in their common commitment to God, compassion, and peace. But, less globally and more specifically, Ramadan unites extended families in their shared faith and joy and peace. Each day, Muslims break their Ramadan fast with a meal (*iftar*) with immediate family but also with large, extended families and neighbors.

My favorite part of Ramadan is iftar but not, as you might expect, because we can finally eat and drink (more like feasting) but because every night we gathered together as a family. As a child, we would anxiously await the call to prayer announcing sunset and then eat a date, drink some water, and then enjoy as a family my mom's delicious cooking.

We would eat, laugh, talk, "fight," compare the difficulty of today's fasting with the previous day's, and then go to pray together either at the mosque or in our home.

By the middle of Ramadan, major feasts would begin. Every day we would be invited to a major family gathering where sometimes over a hundred people gathered together. Some days we would host. Cousins, friends, co-workers, and even strangers would be invited. It was loud, hectic, and sometimes even chaotic. It was our most joyous time of the year.

Again, Ramadan is not just about God and family (or families wealthy enough to throw big parties). Fasting makes the wealthy keenly aware of the suffering of those who lack adequate food, shelter, and clothing. Ramadan, then, raises awareness of the needs of others, especially the poor. As Ramadan increases one's empathy toward the poor, Muslim communities work together to raise money for the poor, donate clothes and food, and hold iftar dinners for the less fortunate. In 2016, British Muslims donated £100 million to charity during Ramadan (in Britain, Muslims give more to charity than Christians, Jews, and atheists do combined.) A Muslim who eats or drinks during the Ramadan fast is required to feed sixty poor people.

By the end of Ramadan, our family would make a financial contribution to those who are less fortunate. Each year my family would discuss who we should make our contribution to that year. I was so pleased when I was finally chosen to deliver our gifts.

Charity wasn't just for strangers. When Eid (the Ramadan Eid begins the day after the last day of Ramadan fasting) arrived, my dad, brothers and cousins would meet after morning prayer and visit our married relatives (sisters, cousins, etc.) and leave gifts for them (usually financial gifts). Once I counted twenty different visits on the first day of Eid, and it lasts three days!

Ramadan was my first serious connection to (or exploration of) a divine being. I remember waking drowsily each morning to eat and drink before the call of prayer at dawn. But after the call of prayer one day, I was so excited I couldn't get back to sleep. That call of prayer included the following: "Prayer is better than sleep." Instead of acceding to the warm, inviting call of my bed, I asked my father if we could go to the mosque to pray. While he preferred to do his morning prayer at home, he got dressed, walked with me to the mosque, and we prayed together.

6

Shia and Sunni

"Iraq is fighting the infidels," I told my sister, firm in my conviction that the Iran-Iraq war was about devout Muslims saving their country from the attacking infidels. It was the 1980s and my channel-surfing had led me to a propaganda film about the Iran-Iraq war. It was half Rambo-style action movie and half soap opera. I was six or seven years old, and my older sister, Najah, intrigued by my uncharacteristic quietness, had asked me what I was watching. I explained that the Iraqis were good Muslims (because they spoke Arabic) fighting the wicked invaders (based on their speaking a weird language). With good guys and bad guys thus identified, I stood on the side of righteousness!

Najah was horrified both by my choice of entertainment and by my comments. She corrected all of my false assumptions. She explained that Iranians are Muslims—Shia Muslims—although I had no idea what "Shia" meant. She also explained that most Muslims around the world don't speak Arabic and that many Arabic speakers are not Muslim.

Najah told me that Islam includes many theologies, which have divided Muslims from very early on, and that Muslims have not agreed on a single interpretation of the Quran or a single understanding of Islam since the death of the Prophet Muhammad. "We are a Hanafi Sunni family," she explained, "but that doesn't mean that other streams of Islam are bad."

You can imagine my confusion. I liked my simple and comfortable world of black and white, right and wrong, good and bad.

I would later learn that Islam includes more than Sunnis and Shias. The world's 1.6 billion Muslims are just as diverse in their faith and practices as Christians, Jews, and Hindus. While 80 percent of the world's Muslims are Sunni, Islam also includes Ibadis, Sufis, and Quranists. Even within Sunni Islam, there is a wide variety of schools of thoughts including such schools as Hanbali, Hanafi, Maliki, and Shafi, to name just a few.

Theological differences, though, are completely beside the point when trying to understand the Iraq-Iran war. While it would be simple to attribute the war to religious disagreements, I doubt that many if any of the soldiers, government officials, or even religious leaders could explain the historic roots of the Sunni-Shia divide (or any other theological disagreement). This conflict was regional and political, not religious.

In 1980, Iraqi dictator Saddam Hussein invaded Iran because of a territorial dispute over the Shatt al-Arab, the waterway that forms the boundary between the two countries. He likewise feared being overthrown by Iran loyalists in Iraq and decided to attack Iran first. He was also hoping to conquer and control Iranian oil fields. Hussein was a megalomaniac who wanted to be viewed as a great Arab leader. Ego and oil, not religion, created this potent and deadly mix.

The war, which lasted eight years, was mostly a stalemate that killed about 1.5 million people; at least a half million young men became permanently disabled.

But what about ISIS? Surely ISIS is motivated in its jihad against the West by sincere faith, right? While this is easy to think, it's wrong.

Lydia Wilson, research fellow at the Centre for the Resolution of Intractable Conflict at Oxford University, recently conducted field research with ISIS prisoners and found them "woefully ignorant of Islam." It should come as no surprise then that when wannabe jihadists Yusuf Sarwar and Mohammed Ahmed were caught boarding a plane in England, authorities discovered in their luggage the books *Islam for Dummies* and *The Koran for Dummies*.[1]

The behavioral science unit of the United Kingdom's security service, MI5, reported that "far from being religious zealots, a large number of

---

1. Wilson, "What I Discovered."

those involved in terrorism do not practise their faith regularly. Many lack religious literacy and could . . . be regarded as religious novices." The report argued that "a well-established religious identity actually protects against violent radicalisation."[2] In fact, it has been found that regular attendance at a mosque makes extremism considerably less likely.[3]

Ironically, extremists act in clear violation of the Prophet's injunctions against killing women, children, the elderly, noncombatants, and fellow Muslims. Moreover, the Prophet repeatedly warned against the desecration, mutilation, and burning of the bodies of one's enemies. Yet ISIS routinely subjects its prisoners to such draconian abuses: prisoners are shocked, beaten, and suffocated with plastic bags, and then they are beheaded, crucified, or burned alive.

There is no single profile of a terrorist. For some people in some circumstances, poverty and unemployment contribute to radicalization. In parts of Africa with high unemployment rates, ISIS offers a regular paycheck, which can feed whole families. In Syria many recruits join ISIS solely to topple the vicious Assad regime.

In Europe and America, cultural isolation is the number one factor driving young Muslims to extremism. Young, alienated Muslims are attracted by slick media that promises adventure and glory in their tedious and marginalized lives.[4] If American and European communities can make Muslims feel like they are part of their society, individuals are considerably less likely to radicalize. Similarly, Muslim-majority countries must welcome plurality and equality to promote peaceful coexistence.

While religion is often cited as a source of conflict, it can also positively motivate compassion, tolerance, and peace. When I worked in Afghanistan, where the Hanafi School of thought is dominant, my family's affiliation opened many doors for me. I was "one of them." My colleagues and I shared theological common ground in our work with clerics on counter-radicalization and peace in Afghanistan. We created a network of international Muslim leaders who would communicate and work with the clerics in Afghanistan. But for their efforts to be considered and accepted by the Afghan clerics and the population, the majority of these leaders needed to belong to the Hanafi school.

2. "MI5 Report."

3. Schanzer et al., *Anti-Terror Lessons*.

4. Benmelech and Klor, "What Explains the Flow?"

The Quran doesn't promote Hanafis working only with Hanafis and hating, for example, Hanbalis. It doesn't promote Sunnis and Shias dividing and fighting. The Quran, properly understood, should unite Muslims, not divide them. The Muslim's commitment to God supersedes any trivial, human-made theological disagreements. We read in Quran 3:103:

> And hold firmly to the rope of Allah all together and do not become divided. And remember the favor of Allah upon you—when you were enemies and He brought your hearts together and you became, by His favor, brothers. And you were on the edge of a pit of the Fire, and He saved you from it. Thus does Allah make clear to you His verses that you may be guided.

My sister Nagah understood these verses and tried to guide me towards understanding that believing in God is intertwined with caring about people and treating others well. Division and enmity is not reflective of God's will. We should be striving for unity and reconciliation.

7

Suicide Bombings

"Suicide bombings are a form of resistance," a Palestinian high school student once told me in a loud but shaky voice. "The Israelis have ten thousand Palestinians in their prisons. They have killed thousands of Palestinians—mainly kids—and you want us to do nothing!"

A confrontation was brewing between the seventeen-year-old student and me. I had to take a deep breath and remember that my goal was not to win an argument but to win a heart. This meant that before responding, I would have to listen. At the time, around 2004, the Second Intifada, a Palestinian uprising against the Israeli occupation of the West Bank and Gaza, had been raging for a number of years, and thousands of Palestinians had been killed. On the Israeli side, hundreds of people had been killed, and calls for revenge were strong. These calls for violence were getting louder on both sides.

I was representing the Parents Circle-Families Forum, a joint Palestinian-Israeli organization of over 600 families, all who have lost a close family member as a result of the prolonged conflict. Members of the Parents Circle are united in their common belief that reconciliation between individuals and nations is possible and even necessary for a sustainable peace in Israel-Palestine.

When I participated in these forums, I usually visited high schools with my dear friend Rami, an Israeli graphic designer and fellow member of the Parents Circle. Rami and his wife, Nurit, lost their thirteen-year-old daughter, Smadar, in a suicide bombing when a young Palestinian blew himself up in Jerusalem's Zion Square. In the attack, two other schoolgirls had also been killed. With Rami and other members of the Parents Circle–Families Forum, I have visited dozens of Israeli and Palestinian schools to share our stories of anger and grief and to say that nonviolence is the only way forward in the Israeli-Palestinian conflict.

This time I was alone at the Palestinian high school, but I couldn't hear statements about suicide bombings without thinking of Smadar.

"Considering what they are doing to us, anything should go," one of the boys argued, in an attempt to further justify suicide bombing. His argument was nothing new—Rami and I frequently heard such sentiments in both Israeli and Palestinian schools. Anger, grief, frustration, and trauma enable people to justify heinous actions that in normal circumstances would disgust them.

A Jewish student once told me and Rami that it was a shame we hadn't been killed along with our relatives. We have been also accused of being traitors disguised as peace builders. A few times, Israeli students have told me that my brother, having been tortured to death, "deserved what he got."

Once this student had finished venting his rage, I asked him, "How does killing young girls bring *you* freedom? How does it advance the Palestinian cause?"

He had no sense of how such attacks supported the Palestinian cause and no strategy for independence. He was simply speaking out of pain, anger, and a desire for revenge. He was searching for a way to rationalize violence, not because it was right or strategically helpful for Palestinians but because he felt cornered, humiliated, and had nothing to lose. Like many people calling for "justice," what he really wanted was revenge.

What does Islam say about suicide bombings? Islam does, of course, offer some theological justifications for violence and killing. Islam is not a pacifist religion, and there are instances when violence is condoned, within certain limits.

In fact, jihad theory, similar to just war theory in Christianity, was developed in Islam as a premodern strategy for confronting the reality of warfare and placing limitations on it. Quranic verses, for example, discuss the idea of a proportional response and permit Muslims to attack only when attacked.[1] A Muslim is strictly forbidden from killing a fellow Muslim; Muslims who kill other Muslims risk going to hell.

Most relevant to suicide bombings, the Prophet forbids the killing of noncombatants, saying, "Do not kill an old person, a child, a youth or a woman."[2] Islamic legal traditions refine the definition of "noncombatants," as well as the rules for just conduct in warfare. One of the most commonly cited passages, which still guides Islamic theologies of jihad today, is from al-Tabari:

> You must not mutilate [the dead], neither kill a child or aged man or woman. Do not destroy a palm tree, nor burn it with fire and do not cut [down] any fruit-bearing tree. You must not slay any of the flock or the herds or the camels [of your enemies], save for your subsistence. You are likely to pass by people who have devoted their lives to monastic service; leave them [in peace].[3]

A similar passage attributed to the Caliph Abu Bakr reads:

> Do not kill women or children or an aged, infirm person. Do not cut down fruit-bearing trees. Do not destroy an inhabited place. Do not slaughter sheep or camels except for food. Do not burn bees and do not scatter them. Do not steal from the booty, and do not be cowardly.[4]

In spite of the Quran's clear prohibitions against responding disproportionately, killing Muslims, and harming the innocent, humans are exceptionally good at finding loopholes and bending rules to suit their own vengeful purposes.

In Islam, the evolution of the idea of jihad is a perfect example. Despite the injunctions against killing noncombatants, legal scholars in different eras have bent the rules when faced with difficulties. For instance, in the late tenth century and early eleventh century, Ibn Abi Zaminayn prohibited the use of mangonels (catapults) in Islamic warfare because they killed indiscriminately and because their use would injure noncombatants. To put it in modern terms, the catapult was forbidden as a "weapon of mass destruction." However, when faced with the Crusades and the Mongol invasions, when their very lives and nations were at risk, Muslim opinion changed. In the 1300s,

1. See for instance Quran 2:190–94.
2. Abu Dawud, Book 15 (Kitab al-Jihad), Hadith 138 (Abu Dawud 2614).
3. Al-Tabari, *Tarikh* I, 1850.
4. ibn Anas, *Muwatta Malik* 21:971.

Ibn Nahhas declared, "It is permitted to place mangonels against them, and to cast fire and/or water against them, even if there are women and children among them, even if there are Muslim prisoners, merchants [among them]."[5]

Another example is Ibn Taymiyyah's infamous fatwa of 1303. Aggressive Mongol warriors had just invaded Syria. Each Mongol soldier was required to execute up to twenty-four people in the villages they captured; with units of 10,000 Mongol soldiers, you get a sense of the carnage. In fighting back, the Muslim leaders faced a dilemma because some of these Mongols were Muslim—they had converted to Islam, and some people were worried about the Prophet's prohibition against killing Muslims. As a result, Ibn Taymiyyah argued that it was permissible to fight all of the Mongols because their actions and lifestyle made the alleged Muslims *kuffar*, or infidels. In other words, the fatwa permitted jihad against other Muslims, under the justification that they aren't *real* Muslims.

Every time a compromise was made, however, it set a dangerous precedent. Modern extremist groups focus on these infamous compromises to justify violence against Muslims that they disagree with ("they aren't *real* Muslims"). ISIS and al-Qaeda used a ruling intended for a very specific situation (self-defense against attacks by the Mongols) as license to kill other Muslims in offensive warfare because of political and theological disagreements (or, more likely, because of thirst for power and prestige).

The student I met didn't know these Quranic verses on fighting, the hadiths on just war, or the rules surrounding jihad in Islamic history. He had simply heard a Muslim cleric somewhere use the Quran somehow to justify suicide bombings some way. By taking Quranic passages out of context, radical Muslims illegitimately preach that suicide attacks and attacks on civilians are permissible. And disempowered people, rightfully angry, are only too willing to listen. Because the Prophet feared such abuses of Islam, the Quran says that the *ulama* (religious clerics) will be judged the harshest by God.

The Palestinian student, motivated by understandable emotions based on real grievances, was susceptible to the wiles of Muslim fundamentalists who abuse both the Quran and Islamic tradition to legitimize suicide bombings. However, the Quran and the sayings of the Prophet prohibit suicide bombings and the killing of innocents. It is important that we as a community stand firmly together against these vicious abuses of Scripture and tradition.

5. Quoted in Cook, *Understanding Jihad*, 55–56.

8

Insulting Islam

On a chilly Friday afternoon in January 2015, I went to visit my parents in East Jerusalem. My parents are devout, practicing Muslims. For as long as I can remember, my mom has worn a headscarf and prayed five times a day. Her Islamic values were central to the way she raised us.

My father, despite being eighty years old and having had heart surgery, insists on visiting the mosque five times a day to pray. I don't remember my dad being this religious when I was growing up, but he has become more devout with time. He is an honest man and is the first to admit that he is not the most knowledgeable in Islamic theology. For him, Islam is a way to connect to God and be involved in the community. He has no beef with Christians and Jews who have their own ways of connecting to God and community.

Our family is big and boisterous, and we can't get together for dinner without arguing about something or other. It's almost a family tradition. We have heated debates over a table full of food, with lots of hand gestures, arm-waving, and laughter. It could be a meaningful discussion or something silly—it could be about what the Israeli prime minister said or did, global climate warming, or whether or not baklava is better with walnuts or pistachios. We just enjoy a good debate; the louder the better. I've been told by American visitors that my family reminds them of a big Greek or Italian family. If you should come for a visit, consider yourself warned!

This Friday afternoon was not much different. When my father returned from the mosque, he shared with us the imam's points from his Friday sermon. His message had been about the terror attack on employees of *Charlie Hebdo*, the irreverent and satirical magazine published in France. The imam was offended by the peaceful responses of Arab and Muslim leaders and the Muslim community. The imam asked, "How could these leaders go to France and mourn the deaths of those who insulted Islam, while thousands of Muslims are dying in Syria, Yemen, Iraq, Afghanistan and other places? Wouldn't it be more appropriate for the Muslim leaders to show solidarity with those who suffer close by?" The imam had also argued that Muslims should stand up for the Prophet Muhammad and that showing sympathy for the victims, people who had published caricatures of Muhammad, was wrong. "Muslims should do everything possible to stop those attacks on Islam," he demanded.

While the Imam's sermon didn't support violence directly, it implicitly condoned the attacks. As you might expect, my father and I began a lively debate about the sermon. Despite working in conflict resolution for eighteen years, I always find it hardest to apply my skills at home. While my father didn't support the attack against *Charlie Hebdo*, he didn't like my harsh criticism of the imam either.

He explained that the world's passionate response to the attack made him feel that the lives of the French victims were more important than the millions of Syrians, mostly Muslims, who have been killed and displaced.

"None of these leaders are marching in Syria, Iraq, or Afghanistan," he said, "but they are marching in France for those who insulted the Prophet. Don't you see how offensive this is?"

My father is not alone. Many Muslims feel that the world values Muslim lives less than American and European lives. As the imam put it: "Yes, but what about the deaths in Syria? Why is no one talking about them?" The countless deaths in Middle Eastern countries don't make headlines in Western newspapers. While people identify and march in solidarity with the death of eleven critics of Islam, saying, "We are *Charlie Hebdo*," they don't identify with the millions of suffering Muslims in Syria and Iraq. Evidently, "We are not Syria."

I told my father that Muslims should oppose the killing of innocent people anywhere, at any time, especially when done in the name of Islam.

I knew my father would be more likely to listen to an imam than to me, so I showed him a video of one of my favorite imams, Ahmad Shukeiry.

In an interview, Shukeiry explains how Muslims who use violence as a response to anti-Islamic cartoons are themselves insulting the Prophet and are in direct violation of the Quran and Islam. In the Quran, the prescribed course of action in response to insults is nonviolent: "When you hear the verses of Allah being denied and mocked at, then sit not with them, until they engage in a talk other than that" (Quran 4:40). The Quran does not command people to kill those who mock or insult Islam; it simply says, "Don't sit with them" at the time of their mocking. Even so, it allows Muslims to sit and talk with them when they talk about other things. Thus, the teachings of the Quran contradict the theology of the terrorists who attacked *Charlie Hebdo*, the mullahs who issued the death fatwa against Salman Rushdie in 1989, and the imams who urged violence in response to the Danish cartoons and the film trailer for *Innocence of Muslims* insulting the Prophet.

Shukeiry answers a common question among Muslims who support violence in response to insults: "[These men] argue, 'What if someone curses your mom or dad? Imagine that they are cursing our Prophet!' [But] so what? We don't live in a jungle. Since when is it allowed for someone to kill those who curse your mother? If you do, you are likely to rot in prison."

Devout Muslims should neither participate in nor support violence in response to insults to Islam and the Prophet. The Prophet is the model for how Muslims should behave. The Quran tells us that when the Prophet was insulted and accused of being a liar, a magician, and a poet, God told him not to be saddened. God instead commanded him, "Let not their speech grieve you" (Quran 36:76). The Prophet must not give in to anger or hatred, or seek revenge.

The story of Ibn Salul offers a more detailed example of how the Prophet dealt with those who mocked and insulted him. Ibn Salul was one of the chief leaders of the Khazraj tribe in Medina, the city that welcomed the Prophet after he was persecuted in his hometown of Mecca. Despite ostensibly converting to Islam, Ibn Salul led a group known as the *munafiqun*, which means "the hypocrites." This group declared their belief in Islam publicly but worked in secret to undermine the Islamic faith.

Ibn Salul worked for nine years against the Prophet and was known for mocking the Prophet. For instance, he spread rumors that the Prophet's wife, Aisha, had committed adultery. His efforts to create dissent among Muslim groups were so successful that Ibn Salul's son, a devout Muslim, asked the Prophet for permission to kill his own father. The Prophet rejected the request. Ibn Salul was not punished for his actions or words, despite the Prophet having the power to do so.

When Ibn Salul was on his deathbed, the Prophet went to visit him. There, Ibn Salul asked for the Prophet's shirt, which was believed to have some sort of mystical powers, and asked him to attend his funeral. The Prophet agreed. Umar ibn al-Khattab (a respected Muslim leader who would later become the second successor of the Prophet) reminded the Prophet of all the things Ibn Salul had said and done against him and against Islam and tried to persuade him not to attend. However, the Prophet said that in spite of Ibn Salul's deeds, he would petition God more than seventy times if it would save Ibn Salul's soul.

These stories, unfortunately, often fall on deaf ears, as Shukeiry points out. Muslims might shed a tear when they hear these stories and admire Prophet Muhammad's forgiving heart, but they fail to realize that they are also required to follow his example! It's all too easy and even natural to give in to anger, hatred, and vengeance, and then misuse one's religion for violence. But the Prophet, in word and example, forbids this. Following the Prophet's example, Muslims should not let Islam's insulters grieve them. I watched my father tear up as he learned about the Prophet's response to those who insulted him. He understood that we should respond to people who mock our faith with compassion—we should generously share our tunics, sincerely weep at their funerals, and fervently pray seventy times for their souls.

9

Love and Forgiveness

M any people believe that Islam is little more than a set of rules, traditions, and practices to be rigidly followed. To be honest, I used to
think of Islam this way, too. I thought that Allah was an angry God eagerly
waiting to punish anyone who broke his commandments. This image of
Islam came partly from the Scriptures that were emphasized in my school
(madrasa) in Jerusalem. My teachers constantly told us that there are two
angels on our shoulders, one recording our good deeds and the other recording our bad deeds. They told us that on Judgment Day, God will weigh
our good and bad deeds before deciding whether to allow us into heaven or
cast us into hell (Quran 82:10–12). Heavy stuff for little kids.

Those constantly vigilant angels scared me into excessive concern for
following "the rules" and into unmitigated fear of God. I was deathly afraid
during Ramadan, the month of fasting, that if I didn't thoroughly brush my
teeth and completely clean my mouth, a small speck of food might get stuck
in my teeth and, when swallowed, ruin my fast. One of our teachers told
us to think about the scalding water in a shower to help us grasp the fires
of hell (which would be a thousand times hotter and for all eternity). As a
child not even ten years old, I was terrified!

When I was twenty-six years old, I attended a Christian conference in
Seattle where I heard a pastor from the Middle East mocking the hell-fire of
Islam. "Islam is all about punishment and fear," the preacher said. "You can't

find the words 'love' or 'forgiveness' in the Quran." The preacher was from the Middle East and fluent in Arabic. His audience was mostly Westerners. Since they had probably never read the Quran, they had no reason to doubt what he was saying. The preacher proceeded, asking condescendingly, "How can we deal with people who don't believe that God can forgive them or even love them? This should explain the Middle East to you."

Both of these punishment-focused images of Islam—my childish misappropriation and the preacher's condescending caricature—are deeply misguided.

Can you find love and forgiveness in the Quran? The answer is, simply and unequivocally, yes! The Quran describes God first and foremost as merciful, compassionate, loving. Quran 39:53 says, "O My servants who have transgressed against themselves [by sinning], do not despair of the mercy of Allah. Indeed, Allah forgives all sins. Indeed, it is He who is the Forgiving, the Merciful." Five times a day, devout Muslims bow down in prayer and worship reciting the first line of the first chapter of the Quran, "In the name of Allah, the Most Gracious, the Most Merciful" (Quran 1). The world's hundreds of millions of Muslims call upon God's grace and mercy billions of times each day.

So where did my younger self and that older preacher, and lots of other people in between, get the impression that God is eagerly waiting to strike us down for our sins?

Such views, I think, come from controlling Muslim leaders and clerics who focus on Islamic traditions, practices, and rules, but who have forgotten the spirit of Islam. While these practices are important and while I endorse striving for righteousness, Muslims must also understand, connect with, and feel the *purpose* of those rituals and actions.

Moreover, some Muslim leaders highlight and even exploit our all-too-human fears (perhaps to maintain their power and authority over people). Those who justify violence in the name of Islam focus on people's misdeeds; they seek to control and punish people, not to transform hearts. In doing so, they put themselves in the place of God—they set themselves up as judge. But their God is an idol, and their religion is idolatrous, even self-worshipful. Since God is merciful and compassionate, his followers, Muslims should be merciful and compassionate.

Motivating by fear is not unique to religion: many political ideologies use fear and hate to unify, inspire, and drive communities toward a desired end. Tapping into fear, anxiety, and anger at perceived wrongs (including moral or social ills) has driven nations to bigotry, violence, and war.

Fear-driven religion is not unique to Islam. It is the tool of some Christians and Jews as well. Jonathan Edwards' famous sermon "Sinners in the Hands of an Angry God," for instance, is strikingly similar to a Muslim sermon I once heard. Both relished the ease with which God, "when he pleases, [would] cast his enemies down to hell."[1] Both graphically described the pain of hell-fire and enthusiastically endorsed God's judgment of human wickedness. Both warned and even relished the likelihood, inevitability even, of human damnation. Christian and Muslim preachers alike seem to delight in an angry God.

Islam, however, holds that a deep, sincere, and lasting faith must be grounded in the one thing that is stronger than fear: love.

In the Quran, Allah repeatedly declares his love for his people and his desire to forgive them. Quran 3:31 speaks of God's love: "If you should love Allah, then follow me, Allah will love you and forgive you your sins. And Allah is Forgiving and Merciful." Quran 6:54 speaks of God's mercy and forgiveness: "Peace be upon you. Your Lord has decreed upon Himself mercy: that any of you who does wrong out of ignorance and then repents . . . indeed, He is Forgiving and Merciful." My favorite is Quran 7:156, which says, "My mercy encompasses all things."

While Islam affirms God's justice and punishment, Muslims also believe that God's forgiveness is almost boundless. One hadith suggests that God's mercy is so great even Satan may hope for forgiveness: "By the One who holds my soul, these will enter heaven: the iniquitous in his religion, the fool in his life, the one that fire would destroy due to sin. By the One who holds my soul, God will forgive so many, even Satan will reach for it, hoping that [God's forgiveness] will grace him."

When we imagine God, we often imagine God to be a lot like us—and we are judgmental and ungracious. We restrict our love and forgiveness to family, close neighbors, and fellow religious believers, often with disastrous consequences.

God's boundless mercy, however, confounds our finite, all-too-human imaginations. And then it confounds our constrictive love and intolerance for those who are different from us.

God asks Muslims to aspire to love as he boundlessly loves, with a love so gracious and so merciful that even Satan can hope for mercy. Devotion

1. Edwards, "Sinners in the Hands."

to a merciful and forgiving God finds proper expression in love and forgiveness. Muslims should be so merciful that even their worst enemy can hope for their forgiveness.

This is the Muslim community we must struggle to build—a community known for its love and compassion, a community known for forgiving those who wrong it, and a community that shocks the world with its boundless grace.

10

Women and Islam

The majority of the twenty Americans in my tour group had never been to a mosque. They had traveled all the way to Oman on the Arabian Peninsula and were now visiting a mosque for the first time. I encourage travelers to visit places like Oman, Amman, and Indonesia to challenge stereotypes about Muslims and Arabs. My tour company, MEJDI Tours, which specializes in storytelling to break stereotypes, had organized this expedition. The magnificent Sultan Qaboos Mosque was the first stop on this ten-day trip.

After a tour of the mosque, we gathered together with some locals to learn more about Islam in Oman. We were met by a group of women who served us coffee and dates. The group, expecting a bearded man to lecture about Islam, was shocked when one of the women—with a head scarf, big smile, and loud voice—started explaining the basics of the Islamic faith. How, they thought, could a woman address a group of American tourists (mostly men) at a mosque in a Muslim country? This didn't fit their stereotype that women in the Muslim world were oppressed and denied even the most basic rights.

Defying stereotypes, our female lecturer explained that while Oman is a Muslim country, women have a great deal of independence and have been increasingly encouraged to pursue higher education and roles traditionally reserved for men.

With wit and honesty, she answered my group's insistent questions about why Muslim men treat women so badly. After all, we had all read about what happened to Malala when she demanded a woman's right to an education; we had heard of honor murders; we had an awareness of female genital mutilation; and we had seen images of women hidden beneath black or blue "tents" (*niqab*).

Our lecturer's forthright and winsome reply was sobering: while in some communities and traditions Muslim women are oppressed, they do so in violation of the Quran. For example, the Quran affirms modesty on the part of *both* men and women, but head-coverings are nowhere mentioned. Their imposition is a later, cultural, non-Quranic addition to the text. While many Muslim women do indeed wear head-coverings, a head-covering is *not mandatory* in Islam.

Moreover, and most fundamentally, the Quran affirms the basic equality of men and women, holding that men and women, having originated from a single self or soul (*nafs*), have a "like" nature (4:1). In the real Islam derived from the Quran, women and men are equal.

So, whenever women are oppressed by Muslims, whenever they are treated unequally or not as fully human, their oppressors are acting in sin, in defiance of the clear will of Allah as revealed in the Quran.

Finally, since according to the Quran there is no compulsion in religion (2:256), men (and women) who compel or force their understandings of Islam on women do so in clear defiance of the Quran.

The Quran affirms that husbands should give special care (*qawwamun*) to their wives (maybe even that all men should care for all women). Remember, the Quran was written at a time when women were socially, physically, and economically disadvantaged (weak); so their socially, physically, and economically advantaged (strong) husbands were commanded to protect and encourage their wives.

Sadly, *qawwamun* is often taken to mean that men are in charge of women and even given license to beat women to keep them in line. For example, Quran 4:34 has been used by Muslim men in vicious ways to rationalize their oppression of women and even domestic violence. While the Arabic term *daraba* sometimes means "strike," it can also mean "to leave" or "to discipline." You can imagine which translation oppressive men prefer.

We can't settle here the precise interpretation of the Quran. Suffice it to say that the Quran favors liberation, affirms equality, and rejects compulsion in matters of religion.

We find Islamic liberation and equality in the stories of inspiring Muslim women, both in history and today—women who are shaping the future of the Muslim world.

In the early days of Islam, women had major roles to play in the Muslim world. Muhammad's first wife, Khadija, was a businesswoman who used her money and power to support his message. Khadija was not an exception. Bedouin women, alongside their husbands, worked the fields, milked the cows, and harvested grain. The Hadith is full of stories of women who were instrumental in shaping the earliest Muslim communities.

Today, Muslim women are scientists, artists, activists, and civic and religious leaders.[1] Eight Muslim women have served as heads of state. In Iran and Oman, a higher percentage of women study STEM fields than in the United States.[2] In 2014, Maryam Mirzakhani, professor of mathematics at Stanford University, who was born and raised in Tehran, was awarded the Fields Medal, one of the most prestigious awards in mathematics. The Fields Medal was established in 1936 and is given once every four years to a mathematician under the age of forty. Mirzakhani was the first woman ever to win the prize.

Muslim women have inspired me and shaped my outlook on life. My mother, who lost her father at age four, is at the top of my list. After her father died, leaving her mother with five children, her Palestinian uncle took her and her sister from Egypt to live in Jerusalem, leaving their three older brothers with their mother. My mother grew up with no access to education. As a child, she worked on the family farm, carrying water buckets from the well to the barn, herding and feeding animals, and cleaning house. She eventually learned to sew, and she sold her products to earn money to help her family. She didn't see her mother for fifteen years.

Despite having a hard life, my mother has always been the loudest voice of inspiration, hope, and optimism in my life. She and my dad saved money to send me to a private school until I was sixteen. She pushed me to study and go to college even though she has never learned to read or write. She would always tell me, "There is nothing that can stop you from becoming what you want to be," and "Education is the key for you to break away from being a victim." She taught and showed me that nothing is impossible and that I should not accept the barriers put on me by the dominant culture

1. "Muslim Women: Past and Present."
2. Charles, "What Gender Is Science?"

(before I was aware of any barriers). Because of her, I love the Hadiths that talk about honoring your mother:

> The Prophet Muhammad said, may Allah's peace and blessings be upon him: "Your Heaven lies under the feet of your mother" (Ahmad, Nasai).

> A man came to the Prophet and said, "O Messenger of God! Who among the people is the most worthy of my good companionship?" The Prophet said: "Your mother." The man said, "Then who?" The Prophet said: "Then your mother." The man further asked, "Then who?" The Prophet said: "Then your mother." The man asked again, "Then who?" The Prophet said: "Then your father." (Bukhari, Muslim)

My father had to quit school in 1947 when he was ten years old after they found a bomb in his school. By the time the war was over in 1949, the school wouldn't accept him back, and his family needed his support. He had to start working when he was eleven years old. My parents are both conservative Muslims. They pray five times a day; they fast during the month of Ramadan; and they have made pilgrimages to Mecca many times.

However, my parents' generally conservative understanding of Islam did not limit my sisters' freedom or diminish their dreams. My parents gave them the freedom to choose their own expressions of Islam and their own ways of life. My sisters were never required to wear a head cover. My older sister freely chose to wear one in her late thirties.

My oldest sister, Zakiyeh, taught rugged, nomadic Bedouins, men and women alike. My other sister, Nagah, was among the first in our family to attend college. When a group of men from the family complained to my father about "allowing her" to study and work, he rejected their claim and covered the cost of Nagah's studies. After graduating with a degree in English literature, Nagah taught in my elementary school and did freelance translation jobs. I admire both Zakiyeh and Nagah.

Growing up in a family that empowered women made me understand from a young age that women are not inferior to men. Men and women are equal.

In my mid-teens, my nineteen-year-old cousin, Reema, moved from Hebron to Jerusalem to work at the National Democratic Institute. Reema, who lived with us for the next few years, was very influential in my life. I watched as she built a successful and independent life, eventually becoming a journalist and a television host. I was challenged and inspired to follow in her footsteps.

These women, my role models, grew up in the Middle East where some men, falsely speaking in the name of Islam, sought to limit their freedoms. They triumphed over such small men.

11

Are Non-Muslims Infidels?

In 2013 my Canadian-Syrian colleague, Nousha Kabawat, and I were running an educational camp for the children of Syrian refugees on the Syrian-Turkish border. We had been to Syria and Turkey just a few months earlier and witnessed the despair of Syrians. Half of the Syrian refugees are children. Millions of them. We talked to dozens of children who couldn't attend school anymore. They lived in tents, and the camp felt like a large prison. Their parents had no jobs and depended on aid for food and water. While we felt helpless in the face of such a large tragedy, we knew we had to do something. Nousha and I invited our friends to come with us to run a summer educational camp, and we collected donations from our families and friends. Nine volunteers—musicians, teachers, photographers, and college students—joined us for our first camp. We had over 400 children.

Nousha comes from a Syrian-Christian family, and like many of her peers, she identifies as both Syrian and Christian. For years she has helped Syrian kids all over Syria, Lebanon, Turkey, and Jordan through her organization, Project Amal ou Salam (meaning, "Project Hope and Peace"). She works indefatigably to empower these children, refugees from horrific violence, through education, intervention, and trauma-based care. Her work with refugee populations within and outside of Syria seeks to recover the "lost generation" of Syrian children to rebuild their country and work for peace.

In one of our workshops, we gave groups of students some art supplies and asked them to build the future country they dreamed of. One group built a school, a hospital, and a mosque. Nousha asked them if they would also build a church. Not knowing that Nousha was a Christian, they responded, "No. Christians are infidels."

As Nousha walked away sadly, some volunteers (both Muslim and Christian) started a conversation with the kids. These kids had been living in a war zone and were exposed to extremist ideology, which easily spreads in conflict zones. They were unaware that Syrian Christians existed. After a short conversation, with many appreciative glances cast towards Nousha, they were convicted. They made crosses from the art supplies and presented them to Nousha as a gift.

Since then, Nousha has run educational camps for thousands of Syrian children in Syria, Turkey, Lebanon, and Jordan. She has started schools for refugees all over the Middle East. She is a Christian Syrian who didn't let the fear of Muslims stop her from her mission. I have witnessed Nousha's work for the past six years and have traveled extensively with her. She has risked her life again and again for Syrian children, regardless of their religious and ethnic backgrounds. She cares for everyone, and those she serves and interacts with notice her dedication. I know that thousands of Muslim and Christian children and adults have changed their worldview because of her commitment and example.

Fear has been instilled in children from conflict zones because of the hostile environment, misinformation, and a radical political ideology (packaged in a familiar religious wrapping). These children were struggling to preserve both their social identity and, literally, their lives. Radical groups made them feel that all non-Muslims are a threat to their Muslim identity and even to their very existence. In short, their very real fears were easily channeled into an indiscriminate hatred of those whom radical extremists called "the enemy."

The best way to fight such fears is to experience direct contact with "the enemy." Nousha's loving care changed those kids' hearts and minds. Her compassion transformed their fears into friendship. They stopped seeing non-Muslims as enemies and began to think that some of them, at least, were friends. The healing had begun.

While the most effective means of transforming fear into trust is through personal relationships with "the enemy," understanding and enacting Islamic teachings about how we should treat people of other religions can also counter extremist ideologies. According to the Quran, God sent his revelation to both Jews and Christians: "The same religion has He established for you as that which He enjoined on Noah . . . and that which We enjoined on Abraham, Moses, and Jesus" (42:13). Additionally, the Scriptures given by these prophets are genuine Scriptures from God: "We believe in Allah, and in what has been revealed to us and what was revealed to Abraham, Ismail, Isaac, Jacob, and the Tribes, and in (the Books) given to Moses, Jesus, and the Prophets, from their Lord: We make no distinction between one and another among them" (3:84). All "People of the Book" can be faithfully submissive to God: "Surely those who believe, and those who are Jews, and the Christians, and the Sabians—whoever believes in God and the Last Day and does good, they shall have their reward from their Lord. And there will be no fear for them, nor shall they grieve" (2:62, 5:69, and many other verses).

Moreover, the Prophet commanded Muslims to protect, respect, and live in peace with non-Muslims; they are to treat everyone with kindness and justice (5.8; 60:8–9; countless other surahs).

Have Muslims ever lived up to the Quranic teachings to live in peace and respect with non-Muslim? Or does history show a lamentable inclination to conquest, oppression, and death?

As with Christian leaders throughout history, different Muslim leaders have taken vastly different approaches to non-Muslims—some are compassionate and tolerant, others admittedly vicious and oppressive. Muslim-Christian relations depended on leader and location.

Some leaders, such as the "Mad Caliph," Al Hakim (996–1021), also known as "the Nero of Islam," persecuted Christians and Jews. He forced Christians and Jews to wear identifying marks (crosses for Christians and wooden blocks for Jews), banned the celebration of Easter, destroyed the Church of the Holy Sepulchre in Jerusalem, and demolished synagogues all over Syria. (He also had all dogs killed because he didn't like the sound of barking.) But the "Mad Caliph," who was probably mentally ill, should not be taken as representative of Islam.

We have all heard of the atrocities perpetuated in the name of Allah by the Taliban, Al-Qaeda, and ISIS. But their hundreds of thousands of members (as disruptive as they are) don't represent the 1.6 billion Muslims in the world.

Admittedly, the Mad Caliph, Al-Qaeda, and ISIS can find verses in the Quran and stories in the hadith that seem to support violence toward

Christians and Jews (for example, Quran 9:30; 5:52). But these texts were written in response to a specific problem with specific Christian and Jewish communities that were at war with Muslims. While it is right and just not to befriend people who are trying to kill innocent members of your community and to defend yourself against their attacks, it is not right and just to turn such texts, aimed at very specific situations, into a general rule.

The general rule in the Quran is clear: show mercy and justice towards Jews and Christians; live side-by-side in peace with fellow People of the Book. In so doing, God can replace enmity and war with love and peace: "It may be that Allah will bring about love between you and those of them with whom you are now at enmity" (Quran 60:8–10).

Muslims can do no better than follow the Prophet's example. In 628 the Prophet Muhammad granted to the monks of St. Catherine Monastery in Mount Sinai a Charter of Privileges to protect their religious practices and buildings:

> This is a message written by Muhammad the son of Abdullah, as a covenant to those who adopt Christianity, far and near, we are behind them. Verily, I defend them by myself, the servants, the helpers, and my followers, because Christians are my citizens and by Allah I hold out against anything that displeases them. No compulsion is to be on them. Neither are their judges to be changed from their jobs, nor their monks from their monasteries. No one is to destroy a house of their religion, to damage it, or to carry anything from it to the Muslims' houses. Should anyone take any of these, he would spoil God's covenant, and disobey his Prophet. . . . Their churches are to be respected. They are neither to be prevented from repairing them nor the sacredness of their covenants. No one of the nations is to disobey this covenant till the Day of Judgment and the end of the World.

These are clear instructions that the Prophet requires of faithful Muslim leaders and their followers until the end of the world.

12

Refugees

Amneh, an eleven-year-old Syrian refugee in Turkey, once told me: "I am so afraid of the sound of planes. When I hear them, I hide under a bed." She told me how she had been shot at and heard bombs falling and then exploding around her home in Syria. She was deeply traumatized.

Her younger sister, Arwa, interrupted. "I'm not afraid," she said.

Amneh said that Arwa, though four years younger, would comfort her and hold her hand during air strikes. She still does today whenever they hear a plane.

When I asked Arwa why she wasn't afraid, she said, "What's the worst that can happen? I die? Dying and going to heaven is better than life in this hell."

Amneh and Arwa, like so many refugee children, don't talk like children anymore. They have lost one of the most valuable things that children have: innocence. They talk about death, destruction, and danger as if these were normal things; sadly, death and destruction are normal to them.

Arwa and Amneh told me that they missed their home in Syria. They wanted nothing more than to go home. Amneh said that she feels guilty for having fun at our summer camp, knowing that many kids are suffering in war-torn Syria and overcrowded refugee camps.

Life in a refugee camp is worse than most of us can imagine. Tens of thousands of people live under harsh conditions for months and even years. Their lives are demoralizing and humiliating. They can't work and depend on gifts of food, water, and shelter to survive. Most miss their past lives and lack hope for their future. No one can leave this prison without a permit.

When the Prophet Muhammad, along with other believers, left Mecca for Medina, they established an example for welcoming others fleeing persecution: they eagerly shared everything, however meager, with the new refugees. We read in the Quran: "And [also for] those who were settled in al-Madinah and [adopted] the faith before them. They love those who emigrated to them and find not any want in their breasts of what the emigrants were given but give [them] preference over themselves, even though they are in privation" (59:9). Believers' compassion towards refugees requires not favoring themselves—they must desire the other's good as they desire their own. Even if they are impoverished, they must give to the refugee as they give to their own selves.

Sadly, Muslims sometimes fail to live up to the Prophet's revelation of compassion: refugees can face hostility even in Muslim-majority countries. This shouldn't surprise us. Biologically speaking, groups (human and animal) instinctively fear newcomers and consider them a threat. Newcomers increase competition for (often scarce) resources; so they are costly to support. Groups fear that newcomers might be aggressive or domineering, or introduce behaviors or ideas that damage the group's unity. Groups, then, are typically overprotective, demonizing the refugee and immigrant as both a burden and a threat.

All three Abrahamic religions knew their followers would face the difficult question of how to treat strangers. And all three traditions give the same answer: show mercy, costly and risky mercy.

Righteousness, according to the Quran, requires much more than turning one's face towards Mecca; righteousness also requires sharing one's wealth with orphans, the helpless, and the stranger (Quran 2:178). One must share with strangers as one shares with one's own family (16:91). One must give to strangers as one gives to oneself (59:9).

The Quran, like the Hebrew and Christian Scriptures, requires believers to subdue their fear of the stranger and show instead costly compassion to those in need and those escaping persecution.

To some Muslims, compassion means that if someone asks for help, you must invite them into their home, care for their needs, protect them from attack (this goes back to more tribal times), and ask them no questions for the first three days.

Such compassion in action was tested during the Holocaust, when antisemitism was at its highest.

Albania, a Muslim-majority nation, refused to comply with Nazi orders to turn over its 200 Jewish citizens. Although occupied by Germany, it also offered refuge to 600 to 1,800 Jewish refugees who were fleeing certain persecution and likely death in Germany, Austria, Serbia, Greece, and Yugoslavia. Government officials, at unimaginable risk, provided their Jewish citizens with fake documentation that allowed them to live safely concealed within its general population. Many of its citizens hid Jews within their homes—caring for them as guests for years, transporting them to safety when danger threatened. In Albania, just a single Jewish family lost members to the Holocaust. By the end of World War II, Albania's Jewish population had increased tenfold!

In Paris, Si Kaddour Benghabrit, rector and imam of the Great Mosque of Paris, forged certificates of Muslim identity for nearly 100 Jews; their "Muslim identity" prevented their deportation to concentration camps. He also provided refuge in the Great Mosque for Jews during the Nazi round-ups. Finally, he arranged safe transport out of Europe for Jews. Through Benghabrit's selfless efforts, hundreds of Jews were saved.

Benghabrit, the citizens of Albania, and countless other heroic Muslims risked their lives saving Jews during the Holocaust.

The recent wave of Muslim refugees from Syria, Iraq, and Afghanistan plays to our fears of the outsider. Western media and local leaders fuel our fears of terrorism and sharia law.

We ask our Christian and Jewish brothers and sisters to call upon the best of their religions to fight those fears and respond in compassion to the greatest humanitarian crisis since Word War II.

Are Muslim refugees, as many fear, a threat to Europe's or America's safety?

Countless studies coalesce on a single conclusion: *refugees aren't violent.* Instead they desperately desire peace and harmony, as they seek to escape the violence that has driven them from their homes.

Between 1975 to 2015, America has admitted over 3.2 million refugees. Only three have been involved in terrorist activity leading to death, and those three came from Cuba in the late 1970s, prior to the establishment of our current rigorous vetting procedures. Not a single person admitted as a refugee from a Muslim-majority country has been involved in a fatal terrorist attack.

Refugees are human beings desperately seeking to escape violence and war. They seek entrance to Europe and the United States because they want to raise their families in peace. They despise the criminal and violent acts that drove them out of their homes. And they do not want to live under ISIS's or the Taliban's merciless rule.

Watching repeated images of terror and war, we can easily to let our fears win. However, it is precisely in these times that we must overcome our fears with faith, hope, and mercy.

Abraham, Jesus, and Muhammad were all refugees and immigrants who were, at various times and in various places, reviled and rejected. Perhaps their refugee status is a message from God that welcoming the stranger lies at the heart of the Abrahamic religions.

13

Is Islam Violent?

"Islam is by nature violent. After all, the Quran says, 'Kill the infidels wherever you find them,'" commented an older man after a lecture. "You're just trying to make Islam look good," he argued, "but you've glossed over the problematic verses in the Quran."

This conversation took place after a speech I gave a few years ago on whether Islam is a violent religion. In my talk, I argued that like other religions, Islam can be interpreted in many ways. I, for instance, believe that Islam has more stories and Scriptures that support peace than violence. But religious texts are often inkblot tests, with readers "seeing" Scriptures as supportive of violence or peace depending on their preconceived notions and failing to see contradictory passages.

I told this man that he was right; there are violent verses in the Quran, just as there are violent verses in the Bible. But I explained to him that if he was going to quote violent passages from the Quran, he should try to understand them within their context. In context, the Quran does *not* say, "Kill the infidels wherever you find them."

I read him the passage that is widely cited as supporting the indiscriminate killing of non-Muslims, Quran 9:5 (the "Verse of the Sword"): "So when the sacred months have passed away, *then slay the idolaters wherever you find them*, and take them captive and besiege them and lie in wait for them in every ambush, then if they repent and keep up prayer and pay the poor-rate, leave their way free to them."

As I finished reciting the verse, he quickly exclaimed, "You see? It says to slay non-Muslims wherever you find them. The Quran licenses Muslims to kill every non-Muslim, doesn't it?"

"I don't think so," I answered. People hastily assume that this passage, among others, endorses the slaying of Christians, Jews, or any non-Muslim anywhere, at any time, and for any reason. They also assume that the indiscriminate killing of non-Muslims is widely accepted by Muslims. Both of these assumptions are wrong.

Before explaining why this verse doesn't mean "Muslims should kill everyone," I asked the older man if I could tell him a bit about my background. I have learned that heated disagreements can be turned into constructive dialogues if we step back from our arguments and assumptions and explain how we came to our current worldview. Who we are, what we've experienced, and what we believe are deeply interconnected, and explaining those connections can mutually enrich a conversation.

I told him that God, faith, and the differences between belief systems had always fascinated me. I learned about Islam growing up, but my Islamic school taught me little about Jewish and Christian points of view. At best, what they taught me were caricatures of Judaism (and Jews) and Christianity (and Christians). This isn't unique to Muslim schools. Most of us learn caricatures of other faiths; we learn just enough to easily refute other religions or to feel superior about our own faith. We seldom sympathetically learn what members of other faith traditions believe themselves. My initial understanding of Christianity was gleaned from newspaper articles and books written by Muslims about Christians. The older man conceded that he also had learned about Islam only from Christians.

Because I wanted to learn how Christians understood the Bible, not just how Muslims understood Christianity, I visited a church and I enrolled in a Bible college in Jerusalem. One of my classes offered principles for how to interpret the scriptures. In class, my fellow students and I struggled with hard passages in the Bible. For example, we had vigorous discussions of texts like 1 Samuel 15:3, "Now go, attack the Amalekites and totally destroy all that belongs to them. Do not spare them; put to death men and women, children and infants, cattle and sheep, camels and donkeys." While this Scripture seemed incredibly violent to me, this class taught me to put myself in the time and culture of the written text. We shouldn't judge things that happened hundreds or thousands of years ago from today's culture and beliefs. Second, we must understand the writer's goals and the community the text was written to. In order to understand this verse, we must understand its context by reading the whole story, the whole chapter, and even the whole book. Finally, we must understand the type of text, the function of the text, and whether this verse was the rule or the exception to the rule.

I came away thinking that God had *not* commanded Christians and Jews everywhere to kill the infants of pagans and destroy their livestock. In fact, I began to think that the text, understood socio-historically, may have been a rationalization of our natural inclination toward excessive violence and not a command from God at all.

And when we apply such principles of interpretation to Quran 9:5, we will see that the scriptures do *not* endorse or approve of the killing of any non-Muslim anywhere at any time.

First, and most importantly, it's wrong to yank this verse out of its context and think we can understand it—one needs to read the verses that precede and follow it. For example, the first verse of Quran 9 speaks of a treaty that had been broken. At the time, such treaties among warring factions were not to encourage trade or establish tourism; they were for the sustenance of a typically fragile peace. In 9:7, we read that Muslims aren't supposed to kill non-Muslims; they are supposed to be just towards them: "So as long as they are upright toward you, be upright toward them. Indeed, Allah loves the righteous." If they keep their side of the bargain, you must keep your side of the bargain—treat them as Allah treats you (the righteous). Sadly, we read that the precarious peace had been violated: the idolaters have "gained dominance over you, they do not observe concerning you any pact of kinship or covenant of protection" (Quran 9:8). In short, they had violated the peace treaty.

A faction violates a peace when its members attack, kill, harm, destroy the other group. Verse 9:5 says that *with respect to those idolaters who have violated the peace treaty and are attacking us*, you may respond in self-defense.

In its wider cultural context, this likely refers to the Arab people of the tribe of Quraysh who oppressed the Prophet, tortured and killed many of his followers, and expelled other followers from Mecca. They then attacked Muslims in their new hometown of Medina. The Quraysh were mainly polytheists, and Islam's monotheistic claim was seen as a threat to their lifestyle. The early Muslim community was thus continuously at war with the tribe of Quraysh. Quran 9:5 takes place soon after the allies of the Quraysh carried out an attack, in violation of their treaty, against the allies of the Muslims. When asked for a peaceful resolution, the Quraysh refused, and the war continued.

If the Quraysh had responded positively to the Muslim request to return to peace, the Muslims were commanded to forgive them. "But if they should repent . . . , let them [go] on their way. Indeed, Allah is Forgiving and Merciful" (Quran 9:5). And if an individual member defects and asks for help, the Muslims must "grant him protection so that he may hear the words of Allah. Then deliver him to his place of safety" (Quran 9:6).

Quran 9, then, permits the killing of the Quraysh *only* if the Quraysh attack them first: "Would you not fight a people who broke their oaths and determined to expel the Messenger, and they had begun the attack upon you the first time?" (Quran 9:13). They are prohibited from attacking the Quraysh, but they are allowed to defend themselves from attack.

Quran 9:5,then, when read in its literary and social context, is a message of peace. Muslims are repeatedly encouraged to seek peace, to respond to attack with a request for peace, to treat those who keep the peace with righteousness, and to give sanctuary to any defector who seeks peace. Only as a last resort, when they are under unremittant attack, are Muslims permitted to fight back.

This is true not only of verse 9:5, but of every so-called "text of terror." The Quran, understood in context, inclines toward peace. In uncertain and violent times, it urges negotiation and diplomacy, with fighting enjoined only as a last resort (and as a matter of self-defense): "Fight in the way of Allah against those who fight against you, but begin not hostilities. Lo! Allah loveth not aggressors" (Quran 2:190).

In times of war, Muslims must constantly seek and always heed the slightest hint of peace. Consider: "And if they incline to peace, then incline to it [also] and rely upon Allah. Indeed, it is He who is the Hearing, the Knowing" (Quran 8:61).

As we've seen, Christians, Muslims, and Jews alike have difficult, violent passages. The Quran is not, as my interlocutor claimed, especially or inherently violent; the Quran was written within a context of constantly warring tribes and factions. The Quran forbids all but defensive war and demands the constant quest for peace, compassion, and forgiveness.

Finally, it must be conceded that some "Muslim" leaders—leaders of Al-Qaeda or ISIS—like some Christian and Jewish leaders—have misused those Scriptures to kill in the name of God. They pull texts out of context to justify offensive wars, suicide bombings, the killing of fellow Muslims, and the harming of innocents. They do so in clear violation of the Quran.

Those who criticize Muslims for having violent Scriptures often ignore the texts of peace in the Quran and explain away the violent Scriptures in their own holy texts. It is easy to excuse or ignore the misdeeds of one's own tradition, while pointing fingers at others. Muslims, of course, do the same to Christians and Jews. None of us should.

Honest conversations are vital for us to overcome these misunderstandings. I was grateful for the man's question, even though many would find it offensive. He asked, and he was willing to hear an explanation that challenged his view about Islam. I don't think my ten-minute conversation with him completely changed his opinion of Islam or Muslims, but by the end of our conversation, he showed an increased appetite to read more about Islam from a Muslim perspective. The exchange was not confrontational anymore, and we were having a dialogue. These meetings, exchanges, and conversations are what keep me hopeful and keep me going. And every one of these conversations is changing at least one person: me.

14

A Clash of Civilizations?

"ISIS is an Israeli creation," proclaimed one of my Syrian friends, a refugee, as we were drinking coffee in a traditional Turkish coffee shop in Istanbul. "They want to destroy Islam by creating ISIS."

My friend, an educated man who works with humanitarian organizations, surprised me with his comment.

"Who is 'they'?" I asked.

"The West," he replied in all seriousness.

I had heard these comments before. Such "clash of civilizations" conspiracy theories are common among Muslims and Arabs and frequently manifest themselves in statements like "The West wants to destroy the Arab world" and "The West is out to destroy Islam." I understand these theories; like my friend, I grew up believing the world was against us.

In school I was taught that the Crusades were Christian wars waged against Islam and that British colonialism and the creation of the state of Israel were a continuation of those wars. On the flip side, I was told that the Ottoman conquest of Constantinople (the Byzantine empire) in 1453 was the Muslim victory over Christendom. These stories shaped my belief in an "East-West" clash of civilizations.

When I first visited the United States in 2000, I learned that belief in the "clash of civilizations" is widespread in the West as well. The term itself originated with the Western political scientist Samuel Huntington.

After almost every lecture I gave in the United States, I was told by audience members, "*They* want to destroy our culture" and "*They* hate us because of our belief in democracy and human rights."

"We" and "they," of course, were code words, meaning:

They: Muslims = Arab = barbarian = enemy
We: Christian = European = civilized = friend

In the Middle East the definitions are the opposite. Wherever I am and whoever is in my audience—Arabs in the Middle East or Westerners in the United States or Europe—I am asked why "they" are against "us."

These "clash of civilizations"—us versus them—narratives are gaining ground: they have become entrenched in the media, public discourse, and even in children's textbooks. Famous movies, such as *Aladdin*, *True Lies*, and *American Sniper*, uniformly portray Muslims as violent barbarians. In the original version of the Disney movie *Aladdin*, the white, Anglo, Barbie-like Jasmine stands in clear contrast to the olive-skinned, shadowy, sweaty Arabs who, the theme song sweetly insists, "They cut off your ear if they don't like your face / It's barbaric, but, hey, it's home." Children, at their most vulnerable age, thus absorbed anti-Arab racism and anti-Islam bigotry. You'd be hard pressed to recall any Western movies or television shows that portray Muslims positively. Media Tenor, a media research institute, examined 2.6 million post-9/11 news stories from ten American, British, and German outlets and found that the media's coverage of Islam is nearly 100 percent negative.[1] Most coverage, reinforced with graphic images of angry soldiers aside devastation and death, depicts Muslims as terrorists and Islam as a source of violence.

As a child, I likewise "learned," for example, that the US invasion of Iraq and the occupation of Palestine are a continuation of the Crusades of the Middle Ages—Christianity's perpetual war against Islam and Muslims. It didn't help that some Western politicians described these wars as "war on Islamic extremism" or that US president George W. Bush called the war in Iraq a "crusade."

Such clash of civilizations stories are deeply divisive, telling us that because we have always hated one another, we will always be at war with one another—until *we* vanquish *them* (when good conquers evil).

While the portrayal of "Christian vs. Muslim" history is both simple and tempting, it is inaccurate. For example, many of the crusades were

1. Bridge Initiative Team, "News Study Analyzes Media Coverage."

fought entirely between Christian groups. The Fourth Crusade saw the Venetians, the Roman Empire, and the Kingdom of France fighting against the Byzantine Empire and the Catholic kingdoms of Hungary and Croatia. In 1135, Pope Innocent II called for a crusade against the Normans, and Pope Gregory IX and Pope Innocent IV both waged crusades against Rome. Pope Urban II's speech at Clermont in 1099 called for war against "pagan Turks," not Muslims. The idea of the Crusades as "Christian vs. Muslim" is a modern creation. The Crusades were vastly more economically and politically motivated—to gain land and goods and power—than religiously motivated.

While the Ottoman defeat of the Byzantine Empire is widely celebrated as a major victory of Islam over Christianity, it had little to do with Muslim-Christian relations. In the legendary showdown of 1453, Muslims and Christians fought on both sides. For example, the Byzantine Empire was supported by Turkic Muslim tribes who hated the Ottomans, while Serbian and Greek Christians fought for the Ottoman Sultan Mehmet II ("the conqueror"). When Constantinople fell, its Greek Orthodox Christian residents didn't blame Muslims for crushing Christianity. Instead, they shouted, "Better to see the turban of the Turk ruling in the City than the Latin mitre [Catholic head-dress]."[2] The Catholic pope at that time, Nicholas V, so feared the loss of power and prestige that he issued an edict authorizing King Alfonso V of Portugal to "attack, conquer, and subjugate . . . enemies of Christ wherever they may be found" and another that sanctioned the purchase of black slaves.[3] Nicholas's sanctioning and even encouragement of violence and slavery was a despicable alliance with power, not a faithful expression of the gospel of Jesus.

These historical examples betray our simple assumptions about "us vs. them." Yet it is all too easy to divide the world into us (good) and them (bad). And those in power have cynically exploited such false distinctions to enlist support for their "holy" struggle against evil (which is typically their unholy and greedy and arrogant quest for wealth and power).

Muslims and Christians alike deploy myths of the "clash of civilizations" to inspire individuals to action and to unify and mobilize faith communities against the evil "other." Al Qaeda and ISIS, for instance, have

2. Haldon, *Palgrave Atlas of Byzantine History*, 161. The citizens of Constantinople believed God was punishing Orthodox leaders for trying to unify with the Catholic Church.

3. "Nicholas V, Papal Bulls of," *Historical Encyclopedia of World Slavery*," 469.

effectively recruited and motivated members by referring to Americans as "Crusaders against Islam." President Bush called the invasion of Iraq a crusade, rallying Christians to support an unjust war that killed hundreds of thousands of innocent civilians (mostly children) and destabilized the Middle East.

Muslims, it must be noted, are not allowed to perpetuate war against other peoples; indeed, they are required to celebrate and embrace other nations and tribes, as Quran 49:13 says, "O mankind! We created you from a single [pair] of a male and a female, and made you into nations and tribes, that ye may know each other (not that ye may despise [each other])." Muslims, then, are required to get to know other people and to learn from other cultures, not despise and battle people who are different from them. The hatred concealed within the clash of civilizations narratives is forbidden within faithful Islam.

God, according to Islam, is on the side of mercy and justice, not on the side of those who call themselves Muslim. When asked whether it was better to live under the rule of an unjust Muslim or a just non-Muslim, Sayyed Ibn Tawus claimed the better choice was the just non-Muslim. He argued that the rule of a just non-Muslim would benefit everyone, while the rule of an unjust Muslim would benefit mostly the leader himself (and harm Muslims and Christians alike). The leader's faith, Ibn Tawus said, is between the leader and God.[4] According to Ibn Tawus, while Muslims may rightly distinguish between just and unjust rulers, they cannot make distinctions between East and West or between Muslims and non-Muslims.

We cannot let these twisted myths of the clash of civilizations fester. They are as divisive and inflammatory as they are false. *We*, the world's 1.6 billion Muslims, are not at war with *them*, the world's 2 billion Christians (and vice versa); we, like them, want justice, mercy, and peace. To release the grip of these false but tempting narratives, we must actively seek understanding, cooperation, and peace, and seek to fulfill the traditional Arabic saying, "Friendship transforms a stranger into a relative."

---

4. Shaharudi, *al-Maraja'iyah al-Deeniya wa Maraja' al-Imamiya*, 58.

15

ISIS and Islam

In 2013, my friend Hasan was moving to Turkey from war-torn Aleppo, Syria; his father had already fled to Turkey. In Turkey, Hasan's father was seeking to rebuild his life by starting a restaurant. Hasan has bold, hazel eyes and dark black hair. He has a witty sense of humor and is always smiling. He was sixteen at the time, and like most teenagers, he felt invincible. But while making the perilous journey from Aleppo to the Turkish border, the car Hasan was riding in was stopped at an ISIS checkpoint. Since ISIS wasn't yet known for its brutality, Hasan wasn't sure what to expect. The ISIS fighters, looking to make trouble, pulled Hasan out of the car and found something to be angry about: Hasan's shirt. His shirt had an abstract design on it, a twist of lines. One of the ISIS men looked at the shirt and said, "This is a cross-like design! How could you wear such a sign!?" When they ripped his shirt off, they saw his tattoo. According to ISIS, anyone with a tattoo is a traitor to Islam.

Hasan was then loaded into a truck and taken to the ISIS compound, where he was interrogated, threatened, and beaten. They demanded that he give them information about the Assad regime or the competing militant groups in the area, which Hasan knew nothing about. The commander, believing him complicit with ISIS's enemies, condemned him to death by beheading.

They took him into a tent, handcuffed him, and stretched him out on a mattress soaked in blood. Hasan assumed it was the blood of a previous victim. A man came into the tent with a sword. Hasan was terrified, certain that his life was over. He begged permission to call his mother, but they refused.

When Hasan had first been taken, the others in Hasan's car told his father. Hasan's father immediately called friends and organizations to find out how to communicate with ISIS and negotiate a ransom. Negotiations began the day Hasan was taken and interrogated. Before his execution could be carried out, a ransom was negotiated with the ISIS leader. Ten minutes after Hasan was forced onto the bloody mattress, his execution was canceled.

Most ISIS victims aren't so lucky.

ISIS believes that they are the only real Muslims and only they have the true interpretation of the Quran. Muslims who practice Islam differently are targets. Christians, Jews, and Hindus are considered infidels, but so too are those that call themselves Muslims but don't live up to ISIS's standard of belief and practice. Indeed, the vast majority of ISIS's victims are Muslims who reject ISIS's radical ideology. ISIS's mission is to purify Islam based on the ultimate "truth" that only they possess.

To that end, ISIS condones stoning, beheading, rape, and crucifixion. And they have destroyed precious and irreplaceable religious and archaeological sites, including Muslim shrines, churches, and historical sites, such as Palmyra, Hatra, Nineveh, and Nimrud.

ISIS doesn't destroy these sites for the sheer delight of destruction. ISIS destroys them because the sites represent versions of religion that it is trying to erase. For instance, by destroying Sufi Muslim shrines and tombs, ISIS seeks to eliminate the Sufi view of Islam. By attacking Shia sites, ISIS attempts to obliterate the diversity of Islam and reinforce its claim to the true religion. By attacking Christians and Yazidis, ISIS seeks to erase non-Islamic religions.

By destroying Persian and Roman sites, ISIS wipes out sites that contradict ISIS's interpretation of history, which includes only two eras: Jahiliyah (the time of ignorance) and Islam (the time of enlightenment). Sites from the Babylonian, Persian, and Roman empires hearken back to golden ages before Islam, ages which don't fit into ISIS's "time of ignorance" narrative. ISIS seeks to control the future by erasing the past.

ISIS is working to ethnically, religiously, and historically cleanse the region through murder, forced conversion, and destruction of the past. It believes no cultural cleansing is complete without erasing all historical traces of infidels. To create a unitary religious state that adheres to its peculiar brand of Islam, ISIS kills people and destroys shrines, mosques, and churches.

The Taliban perpetrated similar atrocities when they destroyed Buddhist sites in Afghanistan. Like ISIS, the Taliban claims that the religious sites they destroy are monuments worshipped in violation of Islam. They contend that they are following in the footsteps of the prophet Abraham who, according to Quran 21:52–67, destroyed his tribe's idols.

But Quran 21 offers no blanket condemnation of statues, even religious ones. Indeed, Abraham himself destroyed only the smaller statues leaving the largest one untouched: "So he made them into fragments, except a large one among them, that they might return to it [and question]" (21:58). Moreover, the text says that Abraham destroyed only the stones they *worshipped*. But today no one worships Baal at Palmyra, or Apollo and Poseidon at Hatra, or Ishtar at Nineveh, or Ninurta at Nimrud. Even if ISIS were correct in claiming the prophet Abraham's authority for itself, they can't claim the Quran orders the destruction of these ancient sites because gods are no longer worshipped at them.

Only by taking Quranic texts out of context, misreading them, and ignoring crucial points can ISIS claim blanket permission to destroy ancient treasures.

Moreover, in engaging in such wanton destruction, ISIS wrongly claims to have the authority of a prophet (Abraham), but the age of prophets ended in the seventh century with Muhammad.

Finally, the Quran praises God-created diversity ("O mankind, indeed We have created you from male and female and made you peoples and tribes that you may know one another," Quran 49:13); affirms the monotheism and prophets of Judaism and Christianity ("Say, [O believers], 'We have believed in Allah and what has been revealed to us and what has been revealed to Abraham and Ishmael and Isaac and Jacob and the Descendants and what was given to Moses and Jesus and what was given to the prophets from their Lord. We make no distinction between any of them, and we are Muslims [in submission] to Him,'" 2:136); condemns forced conversion ("There shall be no compulsion in [acceptance of] the religion," 2:256); and prohibits the killing of fellow Muslims ("and never is it for a believer to a kill a believer," 4:92).

What about stoning, beheading, rape, and crucifixion? Such later cultural accretions—abominations, really—have no place in Islamic conceptions of justice and benevolence. In Quran 5:8, we read: "O you who have believed, be persistently standing firm for Allah, witnesses in justice, and do not let the hatred of a people prevent you from being just. Be just; that is nearer to righteousness. And fear Allah; indeed, Allah is Acquainted with what you do."

In case you think ISIS is motivated by piety, ISIS's leaders are more thugs than saints. They are selling archaeological artifacts on the black market to finance ISIS's military operations. Their atrocities—partially destroying archeological sites—simultaneously increase demand and decrease supply, deliberately driving up prices for their ancient artifacts. Higher prices buy more guns.

Muslim Syrian activists, hoping to counter ISIS's destruction, are working to preserve the history and future of their country. In 2014 I met a young man in his twenties who had infiltrated ISIS-held areas in Syria to document artifacts, preserve sites, and stop the smuggling of archeological artifacts. He has bravely faced ISIS leaders to persuade them to spare archeological sites. I cannot use his real name because his family still lives under the Assad Syrian regime. When I met him, his mother was in prison, put there by the regime. Any news about his activism could potentially harm his family. So, we will call him Ziyad.

During one of his meetings with ISIS militants, their leader, Abu Ammar, called himself an emir (prince). Ziyad told me, "When we tried to talk to him about preserving the archaeology, Abu Ammar laughed at us. He said that he saw no value in saving any cultural or historical sites. For him, the priority was bringing the caliphate and sharia law to Aleppo."

I once asked Ziyad why he fights so hard to save archeological sites, when thousands of people are dying. He explained, "Sites like the Citadel in Aleppo represent our history. We can't have a future if we don't have a past. Our children have to learn about the great civilizations we came from, in order to appreciate Syria's diversity and create a future for our people."

Ziyad is right. We mourn the destruction of these sites and work to preserve them because they are more than piles of rocks: they are a precious, timeless, and yet fragile record of our past. They represent both our

God-given diversity and our God-directed history. When we lose them, we lose a part of who we are.

16

What Can Muslims Learn from Christians and Jews?

Although I grew up in Jerusalem, I didn't know many Christians. My neighborhood was Muslim, my school was Muslim, and my friends were Muslim. Jews and Christians lived in their own neighborhoods, went to their own schools, and had their own friends. My only encounters with Christians was in the offices and shops where they worked; I did my business, paid my money, and left. Other than these shallow encounters, everyone stayed in their own community and lived in their own world. Except for what I saw on television or heard from friends (not typically good sources of information!), I never learned about those other communities and the strange people that inhabited them.

This all changed when I was about eighteen years old. I went to a Hebrew class and met some Jews. And I met a cute, blonde, Christian girl—an American, to boot. I was smitten! One day she invited me, in a strange mix of Hebrew and English, to hear her sing at the YMCA. Since I wasn't fluent in either of those languages and she couldn't speak Arabic, I scarcely understood a word she said. I was certain, however, that it was a date!

When I asked my dad, without mentioning the cute American girl, if I should go to a concert at the Young Men's *Christian* Association, a thing in *their* community, not in mine, my father shrugged and replied, "Why not? The YMCA offers free concerts. If it is free, go!"

So I went. At the YMCA, I was surrounded by many people—Palestinains, Israelis, Russians, Americans, Jews, Muslims, Christians. I sat down, and the group started singing (in Arabic and English): "I have decided to follow Jesus." To my horror, I realized that the "concert" was cover for a church service!

But I was too embarrassed to leave, so I sat through the service, the first time I had ever been in a non-Muslim worship space. When the preacher started to speak, to my surprise, I was moved. The message (which was translated into Arabic) was called, "Love Your Neighbor and Love Your Enemy." This was the perfect message in Jerusalem! Christians, he said, should love Israelis and Palestinians. Israelis should love Palestinians, and Palestinians should love Israelis! I totally agreed with love.

The preacher also challenged and even provoked me. He quoted from the Prophet Isa (Jesus), "You believe that there is one God. Good! Even the demons believe that—and shudder" (Jas 2:19). Then he called everyone to a higher level of faith, one beyond mere intellectual assent. Quoting Jesus again, he said, "If you love those who love you, what reward will you get? Are not even the tax collectors doing that? And if you greet only your own people, what are you doing more than others? Do not even pagans do that?" (Matt 5:46–47). For the first time, I felt the urge to overcome my fears, anger, and even hatred and, in faith, reach out in love to those who were not "my" people.

I was reminded of Quran 4:36 where we are called to love not only our families but also our near neighbors and our far neighbors, as well as the traveler (the stranger, the one not in our community). I realized, for the first time, that Christians, Jews, and Muslims share a lot with one another. We don't always agree, but we are more alike than we think. We share, after all, a deep commitment to love all of God's creatures, not just our own kind. This powerful and provocative sermon inspired me to study both Christianity and Judaism. (As for the cute Christian girl, we never dated, but became very good friends.)

Over the next four years, as a college student in Jerusalem, I also worked in a small porcelain shop in a Jewish ultra-Orthodox neighborhood. I was the only non-Jew in the shop. I found myself fascinated by their prayers, clothes, traditions, and rituals. I recall my fascination as I watched them wash their hands before eating. I loved hearing the ancient resonance of Hebrew in their prayers and seeing the outward expressions of their deep inner faith—their (initially funny) hats, jackets, and curly "sideburns." I started asking questions about their faith, and I was amazed at how similar the essence of their beliefs were to Christianity and Islam. It was not their belief, however, that most touched my heart. It was their actions. One of my colleagues invited me to the wedding of his daughter. When I arrived, he took me to his family's table and seated me as a guest of honor. I was moved. He and I didn't agree on politics, and we argued about work-related stuff all the time. But here, at his daughter's wedding, when it mattered most, we weren't enemies. He introduced me to his family as his friend. Religion, he was showing me, is about behavior, not about belief.

I was humbled and surprised by my colleague's graciousness and the kindness of his fellow Jews. Humility is precisely the response the Quran commends when dealing with other communities. Quran 49:11 says, "Oh believers! Let not one nation (or people) ridicule another nation—it may be that the latter are better than the former." On that day, in that place, and at that moment, I felt, for the first time, the compassion of another "nation." I knew instantly that I needed to learn more from them.

What can Muslims learn from Christians and Jews?

After the YMCA sermon, my favorite verse in the *Injil* (New Testament) remains Jesus's radical call to "love your enemies and pray for those who persecute you" (Matt 5:44). It's more about behavior than belief: I must be patient, kind, and respectful toward people I dislike; I should not live in selfishness or anger when people hurt me. Instead, I should keep no record of wrongs—and I should persevere with them and fight to protect them (1 Cor 13). The world would be a vastly better place if Muslims, Christians, and Jews routinely practiced such behaviors.

My understanding of the struggle for justice was mainly formed by the prophet Isaiah from the Hebrew Bible where he challenges the concept of fasting.

> Is this the kind of fast I have chosen,
> only a day for people to humble themselves?
> Is it only for bowing one's head like a reed?
> Is that what you call a fast,
> a day acceptable to the Lord?
> Is not this the kind of fasting I have chosen:
> to loose the chains of injustice
> to set the oppressed free
> and break every yoke?

> Is it not to share your food with the hungry
> and to provide the poor wanderer with shelter? (Isaiah 58:5–7)

"To loose the chains of injustice"—many of my Christian and Jewish friends have been good models of setting the oppressed free, sharing food with the hungry, and providing shelter for the poor.

Dave, a Christian pastor and friend of mine, was in Scotland when a local mosque was burned down. He gathered a group of Christians to help rebuild the mosque, even when other Christians objected! Another friend of mine, Rabbi Daniel Roth, rushed to the hospital when my father had a medical emergency and needed surgery. Picture this: a rabbi wearing a kippa asking for Muhammad's room.

My friend, Hind Kabawat, is an Arab Syrian Christian who has given most of the last six years volunteering in Syrian refugee camps, supporting Syrian civil society, and working for peace. When Americans began talking about saving Arab Christians from ISIS (ignoring the vast majority of sufferers who were Muslims), Hind traveled to Washington, DC, to challenge Americans to follow the biblical idea of universal love. She appeared before a committee of the US Congress and asked Americans to care not only about Christians but for Muslims, too.

We, Muslim-Christian-Jew, have a lot we can and should learn from one another. Quran 2:177 says,

> Righteousness is not determined by facing East or West [during prayer]. But righteous is he who believes in God and the Last Day and the angels and the Scripture and the prophets; and gives [his] wealth . . . to relatives and orphans and the needy and the wanderer and those who ask, and sets slaves free. . . And those who keep their oath when they make one, and are patient in tribulation and adversity and time of stress. Those are the ones who have been true, and it is those who are righteous.

We've seen that justice is not only about fasting (Hebrew Bible), and love is not only for kin and community (Christian Bible); in the same way, righteousness is not only about how one prays (Quran). Justice sets the oppressed free, love is for strangers and even enemies, and righteousness gives to anyone who asks.

Kelly James Clark

1

Good Samaritans

Over thirty years ago, I was driving home through a blinding blizzard on a January evening in Iowa. As I was entering the highway I noticed a man on the side of the road, crouching down, his faced turned away from the sharp wind and driving snow. The drivers of the six or so cars ahead of me had also glimpsed this desperate man and then zipped by, apparently without giving him a second thought. They were well on their way in their warm cars to their warm homes; they could not be interrupted by this man in such desperate need.

My first reaction was the same as theirs—I was tired from a long day of work and determined to get home as soon as possible. Yet here I was in my warm car and there he was—a stranger on the side of the road.

I was the youth director of a church at the time, and I was exhausted from doing *God's* work. But I had recently taught the parable of the Good Samaritan so, excuses aside, I had to stop.

The parable of the Good Samaritan comes right after Jesus tells his followers the two greatest commandments, one of which is *Love your neighbor as yourself.*

We've heard this repeated so many times it has been emptied of meaning. It no longer seems radical or even shocking.

But it is.

Love your neighbor *as yourself.*

I understand loving myself. Self-love is perfectly natural. Easy-peasy. I can be selfish all day. No prob. In fact, I'm so good at being selfish that loving others is pretty darn hard.

Loving my children as myself—I get that, too. Sometimes I love my children even more than myself. I'm sure I'd throw myself in front of a speeding car to save any one of my children.

We are naturally and deeply constructed to love our own self and our own children in powerful and sometimes irresistible ways. So selfishness I get. Loving my own children, no problem (okay, mostly no problem). Selfishness and love of my own children are built into my nature. But loving my neighbor or a stranger is not.

So loving my neighbor as I love myself is something that I don't get. Heck, most other people are hard enough to like, let alone to love (let alone to love *as I love myself*).

So I'm on the same page as the legal scholar who asked Jesus, "Who is my neighbor?" Who are these other human beings that I'm supposed to love as my very own self? I'm sure he was hoping to get Jesus to tone down God's command by restricting such demanding love to our children and maybe to our extended "family" (other people who look and act and worship a lot like we do).

Like the legal scholar, I wanted Jesus to acknowledge and affirm limits to our severely limited love. I wanted it restricted, as is natural, to my own kith and kin. And not much beyond. My neighbors, people who are somewhat like me, aren't so hard to love.

Jesus, however, rejects the question. "Who is my neighbor?" is a question about *them*, but Jesus is talking about me. He is not letting me first find out if they are like me in the way they look and act and believe and even smell, so that they are basically neighbors and not strangers. Instead, Jesus is looking me in the eye and saying that the problem isn't them, it's me. He's talking to me about myself. Jesus says that I need to ask myself, "Am *I* neighborly?"

Being neighborly is a function of how you care for anyone who is in need. And "anyone in need" is not restricted to family members (people who look like me) or members of my various groups (people who believe as I believe). Should I find a family member or friend or stranger in need, *I* am to be neighborly to them. It's about *me*, it's not about them.

The model offered in the parable is simple: show neighborly mercy (and do not ask questions about their relationship to you). It's that simple. And that hard.

It goes against every fiber of our being to extend love beyond our small circle of family, friends, and fellow believers to the stranger.

But that's the message of Jesus who I claim to follow. And he and his message led me here, to this stranger on this highway, in a blinding storm, in the dead of winter.

So I stopped and invited the stranger into my car.

He told me that he had another 300 miles to go. When I replied that I could take him just a few more miles down the highway, he was clearly distraught and told me that he had been waiting by the side of the road for over four hours. He had just about given up hope of a ride and had considered laying down and going to sleep, his last, on the side of the road.

Fearing for his life, I invited him to stay the night at my house. On the way, he told me that he was a homeless alcoholic and drug addict who spent most of his nights on the street and that he was desperately unhappy with his life and ready to sleep until death.

You can imagine my wife's surprise when I brought him into our home. After feeding him and making him a bed on our couch, I went upstairs to our bedroom and tried to sleep. But we could hear the stranger walking around and rummaging about (through our things?), and saw him urinating off our back porch.

This understandably upset my wife so she asked me to take him to a hotel.

When I went downstairs to ship him off to the hotel, instead of finding him stealing food, I saw him weeping while reading our Bible.

Somehow shuffling him off to a hotel didn't seem, well, neighborly.

So we talked long into the night about his wretched life and his desire to get himself cleaned up.

The following morning I bought him a bus ticket to his destination, and then I called a church in that town. They happened to have a drug and alcohol rehabilitation program and agreed to greet the man when he arrived to offer their help. They asked nothing about him and expected nothing in return—they were neighbors to him.

This is what my Scriptures teach: I am to be merciful to every single person I meet along my journey. I cannot ask before showing mercy about their religious, ethnic, national, or socioeconomic background. I cannot restrict mercy to my family and friends or those within my circle of faith. It's precisely to those outside of my family and friends—the stranger— where mercy is most demanded.

I cannot set limits on who my neighbor is. That's the wrong question to ask. "How can *I* be neighborly?" is the right question to ask.

As a follower of Jesus, when I see someone in need, I can't favor Christians and shun Jews and Muslims. I can't even ask if they are Muslim, Christian, or Jew (or wherever else we are inclined to set the limits of love—color of skin, gender, sexuality, nationality, or ethnicity).

The parable of the Good Samaritan is not about *them* or *their* looks or beliefs or practices. It's about *me* and *my* attitudes and actions.

Inspired by the parable of the Good Samaritan (or guilted into action), I set aside my very real fears and invited an alcoholic, drug-addicted stranger into my home on that bitterly cold night.

I don't recount this story to make you aware of my great virtue (which, in all honesty, is not so great). But the story offers an example of our perfectly natural and even instinctive desire to distance ourselves from others, often for very good reasons. It's often cold, we're often busy, and others sometimes pose a threat to our security and well-being.

But then there's Jesus' insistence that following him means resisting those distancing impulses. Jesus's admonition to be neighborly takes us way out of our comfort zone—we can't be kind only to those who are "safe," typically, people like ourselves (for example, Christian, white, middle class). We can't even ask if they are like us. We are simply commanded to be neighborly to everyone God brings onto our path.

Given globalization, God has increasingly brought Muslims and Jews onto our paths. Figuring out how to think Christianly about them means thinking first and foremost about how *I* can be neighborly.

2

Friends

Jesus may have commanded us to "love our neighbor as ourselves," but that's hardly our first (or even second) moral instinct. Our first "moral" instinct (one that no one needed to teach us) is: "That's not fair!" When my brother got a bigger piece of cake or I was punished more harshly than my sister, I would indignantly denounce my parents' moral failures and hope they would quickly right their wrongs.

This instinctive impulse to ensure that we get our fair share (and, usually, a bit more) is hardwired into us. And though our cry for justice may seem deeply moral to ourselves, our insistent, whiney demands are just selfishness in disguise.

Consider this strange little parable Jesus tells about workers in a vineyard:

> As Jesus was telling what the kingdom of heaven would be like, he said:
>
> "Early one morning a man went out to hire some workers for his vineyard. After he had agreed to pay them the usual amount for a day's work, he sent them off to his vineyard.
>
> "About nine that morning, the man saw some other people standing in the market with nothing to do. He said he would pay them what was fair, if they would work in his vineyard. So they went.

"At noon and again about three in the afternoon he returned to the market. And each time he made the same agreement with others who were loafing around with nothing to do.

"Finally, about five in the afternoon the man went back and found some others standing there. He asked them, 'Why have you been standing here all day long doing nothing?'

"'Because no one has hired us,' they answered. Then he told them to go work in his vineyard.

"That evening the owner of the vineyard told the man in charge of the workers to call them in and give them their money. He also told the man to begin with the ones who were hired last. When the workers arrived, the ones who had been hired at five in the afternoon were given a full day's pay.

"The workers who had been hired first thought they would be given more than the others. But when they were given the same, they began complaining to the owner of the vineyard. They said, 'The ones who were hired last worked for only one hour. But you paid them the same that you did us. And we worked in the hot sun all day long!'

"The owner answered one of them, 'Friend, I didn't cheat you. I paid you exactly what we agreed on. Take your money now and go! What business is it of yours if I want to pay them the same that I paid you? Don't I have the right to do what I want with my own money? Why should you be jealous, if I want to be generous?'"

Jesus then said, "So it is. Everyone who is now first will be last, and everyone who is last will be first." (Matthew 20:1–16 CEV)

If I were to work all day for $100, and then noticed that the person who worked just one hour had been paid $100 as well, I, too, would exclaim, "That's not fair!"

Jesus, as he often did, was toying with his audience. By making them feel uncomfortable, he hoped to disturb their conventional ways of thinking. He wanted to counter their natural, selfish instincts, which often come disguised as demands for justice. Selfishness is sneaky that way, disguising itself as something good.

In Jesus' story, the first hired workers complain at the end of the day, even though each of them had agreed to the arrangements. The owner responds, addressing one of the complainers as "friend," which should change our expectations. Friends, after all, are not only very different from employees, friends are treated very differently from employees. With that one word, "friend," Jesus transforms the story's dynamic from superior-inferior (boss-worker) to equals (friend-friend). Why, after all, did he hire people for a half-day's work or for a quarter-day's work or for just ten minutes of work? By hiring someone to pick grapes for ten minutes, we can guess that his motivation was not to get his grapes picked. The owner, instead, was helping his friends.

Instead of *working* together (in an economy of labor and reward among unequals), the owner was thinking of working *together* (in an "economy" of friendship and compassion among equals). The owner's goal is not simply to gather grapes and make money. His goal is to create a community of friends who share the labor (and the proceeds) while enjoying each other along the way. The friends work, of course, but they also laugh and love and, in the end, share.

Friends treat each other with compassion and grace; friends freely offer what is needed, not what is earned. Friends give generously to friends, above and beyond what is needed. Friends give what is completely undeserved.

Although the world operates according to merit, the kingdom of God operates by grace. Entrance into God's kingdom is not based on merit (being hard workers) but on grace (being friends).

The owner's ultimate goal in the vineyard, then, was not to gather grapes to make wine (although this was a welcome outcome). It was to gather friends.

As with most gatherings, there's often a shared purpose—to wish someone a happy birthday, to share in the joining of hands in marriage, to help a family repair its barn or bring in crops, or to relax at the end of a hard week. Maybe even to pick grapes. But don't confuse the *task*, which could have been almost anything, with the *purpose*, which was working together as friends and then freely sharing the benefits.

This parable isn't about workers and wages. Bosses, workers, and wages, as we all know, is a recipe for disaster. Bosses can be, well, bossy— condescending, disrespectful, stubborn, and arrogant. Workers can be disdainful, lazy, and ingratiating. You need rules, laws even, to negotiate these very rough waters. And you need people and structures to carry out these laws, like policemen and courts and judges. A worker who feels that she is being slighted or another is being favored cries out "That's not fair!" In a worker-wages situation, everyone demands their fair share.

The parable is about a gracious person who opens his vineyard to more and more friends. Since owners of vineyards can make their own rules, this owner decides not to dispense wages according to time worked.

He generously and equally shares his bounty with everyone. The inherent friendship felt by the boss might just spread among the grape pickers. If you focus simply on fair recompense, you miss the overarching focus on friendship as a guiding principle, both for the one in a position to hire and the ones hired.

Viewing the parable in this light, the kingdom of God is not about the fair dispensing of benefits based on merit, but about grace and generosity.

Grace does not demand what is owed. It's the exact opposite—grace shares what is undeserved and undemanded. "That's not fair" justice is about getting; grace is about giving.

When God gives out his "wages" at the end of the day, when God shares his undeserved joy, do you think you'll be surprised by who gets paid and how much? Will you be surprised when so-and-so passes through those Pearly Gates, thinking to yourself, "How could God possibly be friends with him?" And then whine, "That's not fair!"?

Do you imagine the kingdom of God as a matter of who's in and who's out, where the only ones who get to stay are the hard workers, like you, who get up early and stay on task throughout the day—all day, every day? Where only true believers, like you, who have their theology exactly right, are allowed to reside?

Although we sing "There's a wideness in God's mercy," we act as though God's mercy is strict and narrow and pinched; that only a few people, usually people who are like us and believe like we do, are included. The parable of the Vineyard sounds a warning—we will, one and all, be surprised at the extent of God's grace.

Protestants would have denied Catholics entry into the kingdom (and vice versa). Christians have divided over infant baptism, dancing, singing just the Psalms in worship, watching movies, grape juice for communion, and foot washing. I had a student once who was part of a Christian perfectionist movement. He was convinced that only those who are morally and spiritually perfect when they die get into heaven. He was, I thought, astonishingly self-assured of his own perfection (and equally dismayed at my lack). If I get into heaven, he'll be surprised.

This is the point of the parable of the Vineyard—we will all be very surprised at the number of God's friends. The parable, though, warns against whining that this is unfair because grace isn't fair. Grace is generous, expansive, overflowing, unmerited, and excessive.

This, then, is the take-home message: since the kingdom of God is at hand we should, like God, treat every human being as *friend*—with generous, expansive, overflowing, unmerited, and excessive grace.

3

The Desire to Be Great

"To believe you are magnificent. And gradually to discover that you are not magnificent. Enough labor for one human life." In his poem "Learning," Czeslaw Milosz, in just twenty beautiful words, defines the lifelong struggle of genuine self-understanding: the slow realization that you are not magnificent.[1]

Studies show that pretty much all of us over-inflate our own abilities and personality traits. Like the citizens of Lake Wobegon, each of us thinks we're above average (even well above average). We think we're smarter, better looking, funnier, and even better drivers than other people. Men think they're better than women, whites better than blacks, and the rich look down upon the poor; the educated think they're superior to the uneducated. And so on and so on.

In short, we think ourselves great.

And others not.

Here's a way to tell: do you ever sit at the mall and watch people walk by? Each person that goes by, do you find yourself silently judging, in an instant and without conscious reflection?

- "I'd never wear that."

1. Milosz, "Learning," 60.

- "If that were my baby, I'd make sure the snot was wiped off his face."

- "You wouldn't catch me with such an ugly tattoo."

- "If those were my kids, I'd control their public temper tantrums."

- "How could she let herself go like that?"

With each put-down, do you find yourself feeling smugly superior to every single person who walks by? Right, me neither.

If we're brutally honest, each of us thinks very highly of ourself. It's all about *me*. I think *I* am great.

The Gospel of Mark warns that this desire to be great is the biggest hindrance to following Jesus.

In Mark 9, Jesus takes his disciples aside to explain his forthcoming path of suffering: he tells them that he will soon be betrayed, denounced, shamed, and killed on the cross (Mark 9:31–32). The disciples respond to Jesus' humble and self-sacrificial way by arguing over who among them is the greatest (9:33–34)!

When Jesus again tells his disciples of his impending suffering (10:33–34), James and John take him aside and selfishly ask him to make them great: "Grant us to sit, one at your right hand and one at your left, in your glory" (10:35–37 NIV). In their insidious desire to be great, they think themselves on par with God! When the other disciples learn about their request for seats of honor, "they began to be angry with James and John" (10:41 NIV), and all of the disciples argue, again, about who is the greatest.

Jesus is left alone in his anguish: he will soon be betrayed, mocked, spat upon, condemned, stripped, whipped, and hung on a cross.

And all his disciples want to know is, "Am I the greatest?"

The desire to be great is not just about the disciples. It's about us. It's about me. I want to be great, better than you. And I want you to see my greatness. I suspect you want others to see your greatness, too.

The problem with our desire for greatness is that I don't have to look far to discover I'm not the best at everything (heck, if I'm honest, I'm not the best at anything). What do I do when I come up short? Instead of swirling into depression, I tell myself little stories—useful fictions—to build myself up, usually by putting others down. They go something like this: My car may not be as sporty as theirs, but it gets good gas mileage. She gets better grades, but I have a social life. My hair gets frizzy in the humidity and his doesn't, but that's because I have nice, thick, curly hair and he doesn't. They have a bigger house, but my kids are nicer. Even putting down other's kids can feed our desire to be great!

As I tear down others in order to build myself up, these "useful fictions" become poisonous. When I defend myself and think, "My car isn't as sporty as theirs, but at least it gets good gas mileage," this can quickly slip into, "My car isn't as sporty as theirs because they care only about appearances and I care about the environment." Or: "She gets better grades, but I have a social life" can denigrate into "She's a loser."

Devaluing another to feel good about myself is dangerous (the Bible calls it pride).

Pride goes even deeper. If I feel devalued or threatened, I might become dismissive, impatient, and hurtful toward others. I might give in to disrespect, gossip, intolerance, and even violence.

Acceding to our desire to be great makes for a very harsh world because *my* desire to be great seeps into *our* desire to be great. Studies show that people who have an inflated *self*-image also tend to have an inflated image of the *groups* they belong to. A study of Australian college students found that students who considered themselves superior to other Australian college students also considered Australians as a whole superior to citizens of other countries.[2] Americans who perceive themselves superior to other Americans also consider Americans as a group superior to people from other countries. They think Americans are better than other people simply by virtue of being an American (of course, Brits and Canadians and the French do, too).

The phrase "I'm proud to be an American" can become just the deadly sort of pride the Bible warns against when used to puff us up while putting those in other countries down. Individual Christians who see themselves as superior to other Christians often claim that their church is better—more biblical, say, or more socially conscious, or more youth-friendly—than yours. And when Christians consider Christianity superior to other religions, they can feel that *they* are, thereby, superior to, say, Muslims and Jews. This turns Christian belief itself into pride. And group pride can be vicious and deadly.

Consider some representative anti-Muslim comments taken from a Facebook discussion I was involved in:

2. Hornsey, "Linking Superiority."

- Islam is based on the rejection of the joyful Trinitarian God of love, should we really be surprised when they blow up children?
- Muslims are dangerous and destructive to society—all society—and there is simply no place for them in our Christian country. None.
- Those who subscribe to the radical version of Islam are just following the example of the founder of their religion. Muhammad personally beheaded thousands of Jews. Wasn't Muhammad truly Muslim?
- Islam is a death-cult, a political and social system designed explicitly to destroy every last shred of goodness and decency.
- Fools allow residence to Muslims, who, by the very nature of the spiritual bondage to Islam, can at any time be activated into faithful obedience to the demonic cult that is aboriginal Muhammadan Islam.
- Islam is bad and Christianity is good.[3]

There is, of course, much to lament here (and I left off some of the most vicious): Christians telling Muslim
s what they should believe, Christians judging all Muslims on the basis of a few, Christians judging Islam by the worst versions of its practitioners, and Christians claiming that Islam is a demonic death cult. All of them are versions of the last quotation: Islam is bad, Christianity is good.

Given our desire to be great, it's easy to move from believing that Islam is bad to believing that Muslims are bad. Given human pride, it's easy to think that if Christianity is superior to Islam (and one does if one thinks Christianity true and Islam false), then Christians are superior to Muslims. Then we're on to Islamophobia, bigotry, fear of refugees, and lack of concern for civilian casualties in Arab countries.

In the Gospel of Mark, in the middle of the disciples bickering over who is the greatest, Jesus talks about true greatness, and it's the exact opposite of our desire to be great. He says, "Whoever would be first must be last of all and servant of all" (9:35 NIV). In God's kingdom, greatness is achieved not by elevating oneself above and then looking imperiously down one's nose upon others; it is achieved by humbly placing oneself below and honoring and serving others.

---

3. One might get a better sense of the problematic nature of these statements if one were to insert, "Jew" and "Jewish" for "Muslim" and "Islam." The antisemitism should be readily apparent. Historically, when Christians looked down on Jews, it was bad for Jews. And that's an understatement.

Followers of Jesus, then, should not spend their precious time arguing about the superiority of Christianity over Islam and Judaism. It simply feeds our selfish desire to be great. And, as Milosz wisely warns, to learn that you are not magnificent is enough for one human life.

4

Take Off Your Blinkers!

Sometimes it takes hearing the story of an innocent child to help us see the pain and suffering of others. It was through the eyes of children that white South African author Beverley Naidoo, raised in privilege and prejudice, came to see the suffering caused by apartheid. She wants us to see, too. Her children's book, *Journey to Jo'burg*, tells the story of two black South African children who travel 300 kilometers from their home in a small village to the huge city of Johannesburg. They are trying to find their mother, who works as a maid for a wealthy white family, to tell her that their baby sister is very sick. They believe that if they find their mother, she will figure out how to make their sister well. The story is set in the 1980s when apartheid was at its most intense. On this trip the children feel, for the first time, racial prejudice and even hatred, and it frightens them.

Naidoo didn't always see the pain of apartheid. She writes,

> As a child I never questioned why I could live with my parents in a comfortable home, go to school, play in the park and do all sorts of things black children were not free to do. My upbringing led me to believe that white people were superior and it was natural for them to have the best of everything. But when I realised how false this was, I became very angry at all the injustice around me—and how I was part of it. I had been brought up [like a horse] with blinkers.[1]

1. Naidoo, "Frequently Asked Questions."

Like a horse with blinkers, Naidoo could only see straight ahead and was unable to "see"—to comprehend—anything but her straight-ahead life of white privilege. "Blinkers," what Americans call "blinders," are leather patches perched next to a horse's eyes to prevent it from being distracted. Blinkers, then, blind us to the wider reality beyond our normal experience.

Like apartheid South Africans, we've all been brought up like horses with blinkers. If we wish to see all of God's world, as well as our place in it, we have to be aware of what is going on around us, next to us, and behind us. We can't live life blind to what is going on around us. And yet, like Naidoo, we are blinkered by our culture's values so that we can't see the suffering, even of little children, around the world.

The New Testament uses plenty of creative language to say, "Take off your blinkers!" The most famous is where Jesus speaks of the blinkers worn by those who judge others. "You hypocrite, first take the plank out of your own eye, and then you will see clearly to remove the speck from your brother's eye" (Matt 7:5 NIV). Jesus, as usual, turns our judgment of others onto ourselves. In the Book of Acts, we hear of Saul's blindness to those who believed in a radical love of neighbor. On his way to persecute these people, "something like scales fell from Saul's eyes, and he could see again" (Acts 9:18 NIV).

Unfortunately, most of the time we can't take off our own blinkers, and we are seldom aware of the planks in our own eyes. Just as Saul needed Ananias to pray for him before he could see, we often need others to give us sight. We need help from other people who see the world, God's world, from a different perspective. For that, we need to listen to others and imaginatively see things from another's perspective.

If we listen only to those who are like us (religiously, politically, ethnically, culturally, economically), we can be sure that we won't fully see; those who are like us share our blinkers. Injustice and suffering are sure to flourish if we—rich, white, Western, Christian, Americans—can't see beyond our blinkers.

If Naidoo had listened only to people like her—wealthy, privileged, white, South African Christians—in the 1980s, she wouldn't have seen the suffering of black children. The Bible itself served as one of the Christians' blinkers: church leaders in South Africa used the Bible to justify apartheid. They argued that the Old Testament story of the Tower of Babel illustrated how sin created the separation of different peoples. A church document from the 1970s decreed that although "the Scriptures teach and uphold the essential unity of [hu]mankind and the . . . fundamental equality of all peoples," the final restoration of humankind will only happen at the fulfillment of the kingdom of God.[2] They believed that in the meantime, separate cultures was God's merciful solution to the problem of human differences. Thus, church leaders decided that "separate development" (that is, "apartheid") was the best course of action for South Africa.

Of course, "separate development" is just another name for injustice, white privilege, and prejudice.

Jesus called some of the religious leaders of his time "blind guides." He said, "If the blind lead the blind, both will fall into a pit" (Matt 15:14 NIV). Jesus was referring to leaders who were blinded by their own self-righteousness, spiritual pride, and constricted love. Sometimes our leaders are blinded by the desire to maintain the status quo and their position within it. They can be blinded by fear—the fear of change, the fear of losing their privilege, the fear of losing money, and the fear that all the things they've built will come crashing down.

Naidoo said it wasn't until she left her whites-only school that she met people who challenged her. We, too, need to get outside of our Christian-only institutions, Bible studies, friendships, acquaintances, and groups in order to see.

Here's a first step for getting outside, taking off one's blinkers, and seeing the world from a new perspective: read the other sections in this book, sections addressed to Abraham's Jewish and Muslim children, written from the perspective of a Jew and a Muslim. Try to see the world from their perspective (just as you hope they will try to see the world from yours).

Here's a second step: make a Muslim or a Jewish friend. By the end of *Journey to Jo'burg*, the children are safely at home with their mother and their baby sister, who is recovering after being treated at a hospital. But thirteen-year-old Naledi has been changed by what she's seen. Before going to sleep that night, she remembers overhearing bits of conversations of some older children at her school who didn't want to be trained to be servants. She makes a plan to befriend them once school starts again—her first step in taking off her blinkers.

It's curious that Christians usually want people to seriously listen to them, but they, in turn, won't seriously listen to those who hold different

---

2. From *Human Relations and the South African Scene*, quoted in de Gruchy and de Gruchy, *Church Struggle in South Africa*, 69–70.

beliefs. If you believe you should do unto others as you would have them do unto you, then listen. As you listen you'll hear; and as you look, you'll see.

5

Compassion and Contrition

I have talked about how important it is to see someone from their own perspective: we need to take off our blinkers and see the world from the perspective of a Muslim and a Jew. But if we want to understand ourselves better, we also need to look at ourselves from their perspective. How do we, as Christians, look to outsiders? What impression do they have of us? And what can we learn from that?

In 2007, The Barna Group surveyed young Americans (aged 16–19) who identified as non-Christian and asked them about their impression of Christians and Christianity. Here are their six most common perceptions:

1. Christians are judgmental.

2. Christians are hypocritical.

3. Christianity teaches the same basic ideas as other religions.

4. Christianity is old-fashioned.

5. Christianity has good values and principles.

6. Christians are too political.

David Kinnaman, president of The Barna Group, said, "As we probed why young people had come to such conclusions, I was surprised how much their perceptions were rooted in specific stories and personal interactions with Christians in churches. When they labeled Christians as judgmental this was not merely spiritual defensiveness. It was frequently the result of truly 'unChristian' experiences.'"[1]

Christians, when viewed from the outside, are not seen as pure and lovely. Gentle Jesus may be meek and mild, but Christians can be judgmental and hypocritical, and we sometimes inflict our private religious beliefs on the public through political power. I suspect if an alien were to come to earth and learn about Christianity from US newspapers, it would think Christians mostly hated big government, gay people, science, and high taxes (but loved their guns)! I doubt the alien would glean from news reports of Christians exemplifying Jesus's concern for the poor, the widow, and the oppressed.

Some American Christians sometimes ally their religion with patriotism and power in ways that scare outsiders.[2] Think of the appeals to God, the Almighty, in the run-up to the Iraqi invasion (and the lack of evidence of weapons of mass destruction).[3] President Bush called the invasion a "crusade," reminding us of vicious medieval Christian battles with Muslims for the Holy Land.

The Crusades had tragic consequences for Jews. As the Christian Crusaders passed through Jewish towns on their way to battle Muslims, they decided to punish "the murderers of Christ" along the way. When Jews refused the offer of conversion, thousands were massacred. The Crusaders were so vicious that one Jewish town committed wholesale suicide instead of allowing their children to be abused and killed by the Christians. The Crusaders, motivated by promises of paradise, destroyed Islamic holy sites, and, after bloody battles, expelled and/or enslaved Muslims who refused to convert.

Our most recent "crusade" in Iraq has had equally tragic consequences. We invaded under false pretenses, destroyed Iraq's infrastructure (shock

1. "New Generation."

2. This is the most political of all of the Christian chapters. I write this because US Christianity is often viewed, not always without good reason, as an attempt to create a "Christian" nation in ways not unlike fundamentalist Islam and Judaism. If we Christians fail to understand how we are perceived and why, we will fail in our responses to our non-Christian brothers and sisters.

3. Many Christians also opposed the war in Iraq and continue to oppose the alliance of Christianity with power and empire. I am talking in the next few paragraphs about the (not entirely unjustified) appearance of the alliance of Western Christianity with patriotic power, not the reality of all Christians.

and awe), and disbanded their army (creating a power vacuum which permitted the rise of ISIS).

Consider the thousands of Iraqi children that were killed as "collateral damage" by our not-so-smart bombs (over 40 percent of the victims of mortar attacks in Iraq were children). Aid worker Chris Floyd writes:

> Line up the bodies of the children, the thousands of children—the infants, the toddlers, the schoolkids—whose bodies were torn to pieces, burned alive or riddled with bullets during the American invasion and occupation of Iraq. Line them up in the desert sand, walk past them, mile after mile, all those twisted corpses, those scraps of torn flesh and seeping viscera, those blank faces, those staring eyes fixed forever on nothingness. This is the reality of what happened in Iraq; there is no other reality.[4]

These are just the children killed by bombs. While many innocent adults were also killed by our bombs, countless innocent people died from starvation, malnutrition, and disease after our bombs destroyed the Iraqi infrastructure and polluted its environment.[5] Well over one million innocent people have died as a result of the invasion of Iraq. Little wonder, surveying so much suffering and death, that many Arabs and Muslims are angry at the United States and the Christian religion that enthusiastically undergirded this "crusade."

Jesus, of course, said, "Let the little children come to me, and do not hinder them, for the kingdom of heaven belongs to such as these" (Matt 19:14). Our bombs and our bullets, and the suffering we inflict on children in the name of God, are serious hindrances.

Our alignment of nation and religion is often couched in militant language. While we don't use the term *jihad*, our modern warfare is cast in biblical terms of "powers and principalities" ("the axis of evil," for example). We then ally our spiritual weapons—faith, prayer, and Scripture—with real weapons—bombs, guns, and drones. "If God is with us, who can be against us?" gives the phrase "onward Christian soldiers, marching as to war" a whole new and scary meaning.

Christians should be asking, where are the meek and merciful? Where are the peacemakers?

---

4. Floyd, "War without End."

5. Kentane, "Children of Iraq."

The first step toward peace on the part of those who have abused their power to hurt people is confession and contrition. In short, saying (and meaning), "I'm sorry."

That was the tack of Frankie Schaeffer—son of Francis Schaeffer, evangelical theologian and writer—who came to believe that his own inflammatory speech, in the name of Jesus, had incited Christians to violence. In 2009, Dr. George Tiller, director of an abortion clinic in Wichita, Kansas, was shot and killed. By a Christian. In the name of God.

On the day after the murder of Dr. Tiller, Frank Schaeffer wrote,

> My late father and I share the blame (with many others) for the murder of Dr. George Tiller. . . .
> My father . . . [in his book *A Christian Manifesto*] advocated force if all other methods for rolling back the abortion ruling of Roe v. Wade failed. He compared America and its legalized abortion to Hitler's Germany and said that whatever tactics would have been morally justified in removing Hitler would be justified in trying to stop abortion. . . .
> I am very sorry.[6]

It is not just fundamentalist Muslims that want a Muslim world (a caliphate), or Zionist Jews that want a Jewish nation; evangelical Christians, too, try to create a Christian United States (and world) in their own image. But when religion allies with power, the result is always bad (especially for members of other religions). Christians, too, can be scary. And that is how the world sometimes perceives us (and our religion).

According to the One who blessed the peacemakers, the kingdom of God won't come—can't come—from bullets and bombs. Jesus, recall, resisted Satan's temptation of earthly power:

> Again, the devil took him to a very high mountain and showed him all the kingdoms of the world and their splendor. "All this I will give you," he said, "if you will bow down and worship me."
> Jesus said to him, "Away from me, Satan! For it is written: 'Worship the Lord your God, and serve him only.'"

Jesus resisted the offer of "all the kingdoms of the world and their splendor," choosing instead to worship and serve God. Jesus rejected being the Supreme Commander who lived in splendid palaces, attended by slaves, surrounded by soldiers who monitored his empire. He chose instead the

---

6. Schaeffer, "How I (and Other 'Pro-Life' Leaders) Contributed."

much costlier path of obedience to God, the sort of servant love that would require, in the end, that he lay down his life for his friends. He goes on, in the next passage, to preach his very simple gospel: "'Turn away from your sins!' he said. 'The kingdom of heaven is near.'"

The kingdom of heaven commences from humble contrition (turning away from sins), not earthly power.

When the world rightly perceives Christians as judgmental, warmongering, and lacking compassion, "I'm sorry," is the best place to start. We can only hope that those whose children have suffered and died as a result of our "blessed" bombs can rise above their righteous anger and say, "I forgive you."

6

What's in a Name?

While "a good name is better than fine perfume" (Eccl 7:1 NIV), a bad name, sadly, is a razor that cuts clean to the bone. What *is* in a name?

Names can seem to be arbitrarily chosen, then used for ease of identification, say, or the collection of taxes. But in the Bible names express a person's character. "Joseph," for example, means "May God bring increase." Today it's just Joe, *good ole Joe,* whose birth name "Joseph" and any attendant meaning has long been discarded.

Maybe we don't attach much significance to proper names these days, but not all names are proper names. We often name people, especially people we don't know or don't know very well, by their nationality (American, French, or Saudi), or by their gender (male, female, trans), or by their race (Mexican—thus lumping together all Hispanics—black, or Arab), or religion (Christian, Muslim, Jew, or atheist—God forbid!). And then we automatically associate stereotypical properties with their nationality, say, or race. The French are snobs, Mexicans are lazy (yet they want to steal our jobs), Jews are greedy, and Christians are God's chosen people (i.e., one of us). Arabs and Muslims? Well, terrorists, of course. It's all there, in the name.

Spiritually and morally, there's a lot in a name.

We believe in a God who knows us by name: "But now, this is what the Lord says—he who created you, Jacob, he who formed you, Israel: 'Do not fear, for I have redeemed you; I have summoned you by name; you are mine'" (Isa 43:1 NIV). When God says that he knows us by name, it doesn't mean that (unlike most people) he's really good at remembering names; it means that he knows us, our self, our soul, our essence. And we are his—his people, his friends, his beloved. Moreover, he has written our names on the palm of his hand, and he will not forget us (Isa 49:16).

Thinking about the biblical view of names helps us understand why the twisting of names is so harmful.

I recall a student in my first grade class named Bobby Adams. Bobby was fat, pimpled, and unathletic. We boys twisted his name, "Bobby Adams," into "Adam Bomb" and daily dropped Adam Bombs (atom bombs) on him while he was in the toilet. We took any odd assortment of trash—toilet paper, paper towels, dirt, used chewing gum, pencils, and erasers—and rained down terror, over the top of his toilet stall, onto the vulnerable and defenseless Bobby Adams. There was no fear of retaliation because Bobby was powerless. This "war" was lopsided: all of the boys in the class on one side and hapless Bobby on the other. No Adam Bombs were ever lobbed our way. This was no war though. It was bullying, plain and simple. Perhaps we caused Bobby Adams to hate his own name.

If I'm not mistaken about human nature, your first grade class had a "Bobby Adams," too. And members of your class (perhaps you, too) made his or her life miserable.

I recount this story with no relish and with great shame. I don't remember many things that happened in first grade. I can't even remember the names of my first grade teacher or my best friend. But I fully remember contributing to the demise of Bobby Adams. We were only six or seven years old, "innocent" little kids, yet old enough to invent Adam Bombs to drop onto the undeserving Bobby Adams. Old enough to twist names in ways that hurt.

Our parents told us that sticks and stones can break bones but words would never hurt us. But our parents were wrong. Sticks and stones break bones, *and* words can hurt us. Even more: hurtful words, rhetoric, and ideas can lead to harmful actions.

When you hear the word *Arab*, do you picture a dark-skinned man with a full beard and a towel on his head? Do you picture him riding a camel or driving a cab? When you see an unnamed Arab do you think to yourself, "Abdul" or "Muhammad" (and chuckle inside at their weird names)? When you hear the word *Muslim*, do you automatically but unselfconsciously add "terrorist"? When you think of yourself as an "American," do you feel proud, superior, and civilized (looking down, perhaps, at uncivilized, inferior Middle Eastern countries)?

In 2010 television and radio host Glenn Beck sensationally reported to his audience of millions that 10 percent of Muslims are terrorists. The real figure is less than 1 percent. In fact, it's considerably less than 1 percent, more like 0.0001 percent, thousands of times less than Beck's estimate. He was trying to cement the terms *Muslim* and *terrorist* together in our brain. Not that we needed his help.

After 9/11, "Muslim" and "terrorist" leap together in our minds, without conscious thought or effort. We feel justified, buoyed by our (false) belief that while not all Muslims are terrorists, at least recently, all terrorists are Muslims.[1] Better safe than sorry when it comes to Arabs and Muslims.

In the charming and whimsical Disney film *Aladdin*, Arabs are portrayed as dark, scary, and villainous. In the original release of the film in 1992, these lyrics were sung in the opening song:

> Oh, I come from a land, from a faraway place
> Where the caravan camels roam,
> Where they cut off your ear if they don't like your face
> It's barbaric, but, hey, it's home.

Unlike those barbaric, ear-slicing Arabs, the heroes in the film, Aladdin and Jasmine, are depicted as light-skinned, civilized Anglos. And that's just one film. Add to that the plethora of unshaven, sweaty, and shadowy Arab villains on television and in movies, pile on media images of Muslim extremists and their horrendous carnage, and you get an uninterrupted image of evil Arabs.

But there's a great deal of moral and spiritual harm in associating terror with the names Muslim/Arab or Abdul/Muhammad.

Media-infused images of Muslims and Arabs as evil, barbaric, and violent (by nature or by religion) incite both fear and violence on our part. If Muslims are evil, they should be forced to leave our country, or banned from entering, or carpet-bombed out of existence.

Jesus denounced the prejudices attached to names—prejudices that harmed, for example, Samaritans and lepers and women. I suppose, most interestingly, the Son of God sought out the company of sinners. Instead of acceding to prejudice, he said to his flawed followers, "No longer do I

---

1. It has been shown that non-Muslims carry out vastly more terrorist attacks on US soil than Muslims. Washington's Blog, "Non-Muslims Carried Out."

call you slaves . . . I have called you friends" (John 15:15 NASB). Here's the thing: 100 percent of us were slaves (to sin) yet Jesus refused to view us as slaves, thus creating God's kingdom of friends. But since 99.999 percent of Muslims are *not* terrorists, when we call them terrorists, we perpetuate the sinful earthly kingdom of fear, anger, and even violence.

Jesus calls his followers to seek out those who are hurt by prejudices simply because of the fear conjured up by their name. Find those people, as Jesus did, and love them. Love them, as God does, by their real name, the one God has written on his hand.

7

Pride and Prejudice

W̲e routinely play and win the pride game when we put down people based on clothing, hair styles, tattoos, education, political views, skin color, wealth, children, snotty noses, and even religion. There's always something. Unwittingly and in the blink of an eye, we put every other person down to elevate ourself. It's pride, pure and simple (and, according to the Bible, deadly).

Jesus, however, rejected this competitive form of pride (which takes many different cultural forms) and the prejudice it engenders. Jesus lived in first-century Palestine, in a culture with well-defined roles and rigid hierarchies—each of which consisted of clearly ordered rankings and divisions of prestige and power. Those at the top of the cultural power rankings had a pride problem. Look at how people were valued in his time:

- There was the *social* pecking order: men at the top in the family and society; women hidden behind the scenes; children at the bottom.

- There was the *civic* pecking order: Roman citizens held special privileges not granted to noncitizens (denied to foreigners—barbarians— and slaves).

- There was the *political* pecking order: the emperor at the top; kings, senators, and Roman citizens in the middle; and everyone else at the bottom.

- There was the *economic* pecking order: wealthy men and property owners at the top; lower-class workers in the middle; slaves and outcasts (such as lepers) at the bottom.

- There was a *religious* pecking order: the Jewish community placed the children of Abraham at the top, of course, with non-Jews (gentiles) at the bottom.

- There was even a *Jewish* pecking order: the high priest at the top; the Sanhedrin, Pharisees, Sadducees, and judges in the middle; and ordinary Jews at the bottom.

If you were a rich, male, Roman citizen, you were really something. If you were a poor, non-Jewish woman, too bad for you. Jews would pray, "Thank God I was not born a woman." If you were Jewish, you thought yourself better than gentiles, and if you were a Pharisee, you thought yourself better than ordinary Jews. (The Pharisee stood by himself and prayed, "Thank God I'm not like other people.") Some people were considered by nature suited to be slaves.

In word and deed, Jesus challenged these prevailing pride-and-power structures. He hung out with children. He talked publicly with women— even non-Jewish women. He fed the poor and needy. He criticized lawyers, politicians, and religious leaders. He ate with stinky fishermen and greedy tax collectors. He spoke up for widows and orphans. He was a friend to prostitutes and prisoners. And he said crazy, anti-pride things, like:

- The last shall be first.
- Let the little children come to me.
- Sell everything you have and give to the poor.
- Whoever wants to become great among you must be your servant.

The kingdom of God, Jesus taught, is unlike any other kingdom. In God's kingdom everything is all topsy-turvy: the last are first, the humble are exalted, the king lays down his life for his subjects.

Jesus said that babies, the lowest in any pecking order, are the model citizens of his kingdom. He said, "Let the little children come to me, and do not hinder them, for the kingdom of God belongs to such as these. Truly I tell you, anyone who will not receive the kingdom of God like a little child will never enter it" (Luke 18:16–17 NIV). The kingdom of God is not for the powerful, the bright, the successful, the famous, the rich, or the pious. You can't enter this kingdom by relying on your power or your position, your brains or your brawn, your fashion or your friends. Entrance into this kingdom is in decided opposition to one's social status.

Why a little child? A little child's sense of self is not due to his or her prideful sense of place in some artificial, social hierarchy (attained at the expense of others). Rather, a child is utterly dependent on her parents. Her healthy sense of self is established through the love, joy, and acceptance freely given by her parents.

A child of God is utterly dependent on God for her self-worth, which is established through God's love, joy, and acceptance. Clinging to one's place in some artificial, social hierarchy (one that elevates oneself above those that are judged culturally beneath one in various ways) as a measure of one's worth is contrary to being a child of God. The prideful assertion of our worth to God based on wealth, looks, social status, race, or even religion is, according to the Gospels, deadly.

Indeed, becoming a child would erase all of those artificial and prideful and harmful distinctions. Since children are initially unaffected by their social hierarchy, little children accept everyone as equal.

Consider the racial pecking order, which, in our society favors whites. Children are not born biased toward, say, white people and prejudiced against, say, black people or Arabs. Prejudice is learned (sadly, very early on). Go online and take a so-called "implicit bias" test—one on "Arab-Muslim" or "Race."[1] Go ahead, set this book down, and take a test. I can wait! Trust me, they're worth taking.

Waiting . . .

If you took a test, you probably found out that, despite your best intentions, you are prejudiced against Arabs, Muslims, and African Americans. I know, I took the tests and despite my best intentions found out that I was prejudiced against Arabs, Muslims, and African Americans. Our culture's hierarchy has so deeply penetrated our psyche that we all, no matter our race, judge whites and Westerners at the top, and we judge Arabs, Muslims, and African Americans beneath them.

Little children, on the other hand, "pass" implicit bias tests with flying colors. If children take such tests early enough, before their culture's

1. Project Implicit, 2011.

prejudices have seeped into their souls, they are not biased against Arabs, Muslims, or African Americans. We *learn* pride and prejudice (and the specific shapes they take in one's own culture)

As Christians, then, we have to unlearn pride and prejudice (and reject the hierarchies that embed them) if we are to enter like children into the kingdom of God.

Later in the book of Luke, we read a story of a greedy, powerful man who became like a child. Zacchaeus (that famously short tax collector) is so drawn to Jesus that when he can't catch a glimpse of Jesus walking on the road because of the crowd, he runs ahead and climbs up a tree (like a child) to see him (Luke 19:1–9). When Jesus arrives at Zacchaeus's tree, Jesus stops, chats with Zacchaeus, and then invites himself to dinner. Zacchaeus climbed down and "welcomed him gladly" (19:6 NIV) Zacchaeus has the childlike enthusiasm required for entry into the kingdom of God.

After dinner, without being asked, Zacchaeus offers his money to the poor and says that he will pay back four times over any money he's stolen. Zacchaeus is so excited that he says, "Look, Lord!," just as a child might say to her parents when she wants them to watch her turn a cartwheel: "Look, Mommy, look!"

Jesus's response? "Today salvation has come to this house, because this man, too, is a son of Abraham."

A greedy and despised tax collector from first-century Palestine is now a child of Abraham.

Suppose you, like me, are a white, middle-class American Christian who lives in the wealthiest, most powerful country on earth (heck, the most powerful country in history); you, like me, believe that we are at the top of the dominance hierarchy towering over those of different colors, races, religions, or nations. We sometimes think God got a pretty good deal with us. This self-confidence is a destructive illusion—it's a lie, creating a false sense of self and our place in the cosmos (with "unworthy" people beneath us). Jesus calls us to topple the dominance hierarchies we live in—they are in opposition to his kingdom. To enter his kingdom, we must enter as a child.

We gain our true sense of self, our real place in the cosmos, by first renouncing the destructive delusion that ranks people, religions, and nations from top to bottom (and which self-righteously assures us of our place at the top of those hierarchies). In God's kingdom there is no hierarchy. Pride in our self, our race, our religion, and our nation, and the prejudice it engenders against women, blacks, Arabs, Muslims, and Middle Easterners have no place in the kingdom of God.

Since in God's kingdom it's all going to get flipped anyway, my advice: shoot for the bottom.

8

Love Your Enemies

It's one thing to love friendly neighbors and care for needy strangers but, for God's sake (pun intended), love our *enemies*? All this talk of compassion and tolerance seems trite and even silly when we consider some of the harsh realities of living in the real world. For example, the Chinese government persecutes Christians, and in most Muslim-majority countries Christians live in fear as confessing belief in the Trinity or converting from Islam to Christianity is punishable by death. Are Chinese or Iranian Christians really supposed to love their persecutors and possible killers? What about those who are bent on our destruction? Isn't there a time to fight, even a time to kill, as the writer of Ecclesiastes commends? There is, the author writes, "an appointed time for everything." Wouldn't now be a good time to hate? If we leave out all the warm and fuzzy "time to heal" and "time to laugh" stuff in Ecclesiastes 3, we get a pretty harsh view of reality. Omit those happy-clappy, dancing, and embracing parts, and we read there is a time to die, a time to uproot what is planted, a time to kill, a time to tear down, a time to weep, a time to throw stones, a time to shun, a time to hate (I knew it!), even a time for war. The author of Ecclesiastes knows how the world works—sometimes we have to defend ourselves and protect our loved ones. I mean, really, "love our enemies"?

Jesus doesn't say much about "enemies," but when he does . . .

In the Sermon on the Mount, he says: "You have heard that it was said, 'Love your neighbor and hate your enemy.' But I tell you, love your enemies and pray for those who persecute you" (Matt 5:43–44 NIV).

Love your enemies? Pray for those who persecute you?

What could Jesus possibly have meant? Surely not the obvious: love your enemies. He must have meant something really deep and different (something that doesn't involve actually loving enemies). After all, the world is not a safe place. We must protect ourselves with the occasional war and self-defense. The ever practical and wise Jesus surely would not be saying something so naïve as, "Love your enemies." Surely he meant something like, love your family and your brothers and sisters in Christ.

I suspect Jesus realized that his followers would need some help figuring this one out. So he clarified that love must extend well beyond kith and kin: "If you love those who love you, what reward will you get? Are not even the tax collectors doing that? And if you greet only your own people, what are you doing more than others? Do not even pagans do that?" We're called to go way beyond tax collector love and pagan love—we can't love only our own people. We have to love strangers and even enemies.

He goes on to tell us that our love should be like the Father's love; God causes the sun to rise and the rain to fall on the righteous and the unrighteous. These, of course, are metaphors without much meaning for most of us in our tame world of sunscreen and umbrellas. But to a society of farmers and shepherds, where one's very survival depends on sunshine and rain, sunshine and rain are great goods. God, to get to the point, loves everyone, good and bad (friend and enemy, to get back to Jesus). God's love does not discriminate.

While we sometimes use our Christian beliefs to identify our "enemies"—Muslims, say, or atheists—Jesus himself didn't consider a single human being his enemy. Just as Jesus' listeners needed to learn who their neighbor was (anyone in need), they needed to unlearn who their enemy was (someone worthy of love).

John Lewis, a follower of Jesus, had many enemies but none of his own choosing. He grew up a poor, black boy in rural Alabama in the 1940s and 1950s. As a young adult, he was put in jail forty times, but not because he was a criminal; he was a leader of the civil rights movement. During the first attempted march from Selma to Montgomery on March 7, 1965, Lewis was in the front row of protesters. As they crossed Edmund Pettus Bridge, he was attacked by Alabama state troopers who fractured his skull.

Looking back on that day, he said, "I was prepared to accept the violence, the beating. And I thought we were going to be arrested and simply taken to jail. I didn't have any idea that we would be [met by] state troopers and horses and a posse of the sheriff, that we would be trampled by horses and tear-gassed and beaten all the way back to the church. I thought I was going to die. I thought I saw death. I thought it was my last non-violent protest."[1] If anyone had good cause not to love his enemies, it was Lewis.

Prior to that march, Lewis learned from other civil rights leaders about nonviolent protest, studying Gandhi and learning about Jesus. They practiced how to act in tense situations: they were taught to maintain eye contact, to stand with dignity, and to speak graciously even if they were getting the crap beaten out of them; these were the real WWJD people. Lewis explains why: "In the bosom of every human being there is the spark of the divine. So you don't have a right as a human to abuse that spark of the divine in your fellow human being. . . . If you see someone attacking you, beating you, spitting on you, you have to think of that person—years ago that person was an innocent child, an innocent little baby. And so what happened? Did something go wrong? Did someone teach that person to hate, to abuse others? So you try to appeal to the goodness of every human being. And you don't give up. You never give up on anyone."[2]

In 1987, Lewis was elected to the US House of Representatives from Georgia and has served his country for thirty years. He says, "In all of the years since [the beating] I've not had any sense of bitterness or ill feeling toward any of the people. I just don't have it."[3] Lewis had learned to love his enemies. And his peaceful protest, grounded in love, won!

On March 2, 2013, John Lewis received a public apology from an Alabama police chief for the police's failure to protect Lewis and other Freedom Riders on a bus trip to Montgomery, more than fifty years earlier. When the officer offered Lewis his badge as a sign of trust and respect, Lewis was brought to tears.

If we take Jesus at his word, as John Lewis did, then we do what Jesus commanded us to do for our enemies: pray for them and love them (which, as it did for Lewis, takes arduous reflection and training).

That's it. Those are his only commands regarding enemies.

1. "John Lewis."
2. "John Lewis."
3. "John Lewis."

The Apostle Paul continues Jesus's crazy idea in Romans 12:19–20: "Do not take revenge. . . . On the contrary: 'If your enemy is hungry, feed him; if he is thirsty, give him something to drink. In doing this, you will heap burning coals on his head.'" Paul, quoting Solomon from the book of Proverbs, tells us to kill 'em with kindness: learn what they need, then meet that need. Are they hungry? Give 'em food. Are they thirsty? Give 'em drink. Do they want to build a mosque? Welcome them to the neighborhood and make sure they're allowed to build it. Maybe even pick up a hammer and pound some nails.

Don't be fooled, though: praying for your enemies is just plain hard. You'll have to engage your imagination to empathize with someone you don't understand, someone who looks different than you and worships differently from you. You may have to creatively imagine their fears: Do you frighten them? Do your beliefs and values threaten their way of life? Do you represent a changing world? Does this trouble them? Is your country harming them?

If you can engage with your enemy, person-to-person, and see them as possessing "the spark of the divine," as John Lewis says, and never give up on them, then there might even be reconciliation. That's the genius of Jesus' teaching on loving one's enemies. Regarding enemies, Jesus didn't talk about

> killing them
> or persecuting them
> or shunning them
> or even tolerating them
> all the while, keeping them at a distance.

He said to love them and to pray for them.

Paul said to give your enemies

> food
> drink
> whatever they need.

Do it long enough, then, maybe, your enemy will become your friend.

9

Conspiracies of Decency

———————

One cold January day, I saw from afar the smokestacks at the New England Holocaust Memorial. I had just walked from Boston's North End, after viewing Copp's Hill Burying Ground and the Old North Church, and was headed toward the shopping district, when I saw six smoke stacks rising fifty feet, each one an identical tower of glass and steel. I felt drawn to the structures, and when I got closer I followed the walkway leading into the first tower, which now seemed more like a tall, transparent elevator shaft. I stood alone inside the tower—and looked up. The glass appeared to be frosted. Looking closer, I discovered that the frosty appearance came from tiny lines of seven-digit numbers etched into the glass, all the way from the ground to the sky—a million of them. One million unique, seven-digit numbers etched into each tower. Six million in all. You get it.

Looking down I saw steam rising through the grating at my feet. Beneath the grate was blackness with just a few flecks of light. I walked inside each tower/smoke stack and saw that each was labeled with the name of an extermination camp. Between the towers labeled Sobibor and Auschwitz-Birkenau was a plaque that said, "At the end of the War, 99% of Denmark's Jews were still alive." Given the vastness of these monuments to death, I wondered how that was possible. I knew that Poland had lost more than 90 percent of its Jews. What was so different about Denmark and the Danes?

The short description said that the Danish people had ferried 7,800 Jews across the water to Sweden. That tantalizing fact did little more than whet my appetite.

I later discovered that Denmark's remarkable success in protecting its Jewish citizens started hundreds of years ago. In the fifteenth century, Jews were invited by Denmark's king to settle in Denmark. In 1814, they were granted civic equality, and in 1849 they were given full rights as citizens. By the 1930s, Jews had been fully integrated into all areas of Danish society for nearly a century; many were leaders in society.[1]

Why Denmark, of all places, and not Germany? In the nineteenth century, Nicolai F. S. Grundtvig inspired his country to pursue a popular democracy by encouraging independent thinking and fostering creativity. Grundtvig was a Christian theologian, a historian, an educator, and a poet with profound humanitarian beliefs that can be summed up in his famous quotation: "First a human—then a Christian."[2] By the time of the German invasion of Denmark, the Danish national character, based on this egalitarian mind-set, was fixed.

When Germany occupied Denmark in 1940, the Danish government instituted a policy of cooperation with the Nazis, but they made clear that they would not tolerate any actions against Danish Jews. From the very beginning of the occupation, resistance workers sprang up all over. Students and journalists published underground newspapers, housewives listened to the BBC and translated the stories for the underground newspapers, and even small children helped by delivering the newspapers. Those who could not participate contributed money to the resistance.[3]

In September 1943, sympathetic Germans in strategic leadership positions warned that Danish Jews would soon be arrested and deported. Immediately, thousands of people spontaneously moved to protect their neighbors, either by hiding them or by helping them get to the coast in order to escape across the Øresund (the strait that separates Denmark and Sweden). Seventeen-year-old Robert Pedersen went from house to house looking for nameplates with Jewish-sounding names and notified families of the deportation. Headmasters warned their Jewish students. A piano teacher warned her fourteen-year-old student, the daughter of a

1. "Denmark Virtual Jewish History Tour."
2. Jespersen, *History of Denmark*, 113.
3. Werner, *Conspiracy of Decency*, 22–23.

Copenhagen rabbi.[4] An informal underground system immediately developed as Jewish families fled to the coast, needing shelter until a boat could take them to Sweden. Many Jews were told to go to the local hospital carrying a small bouquet of flowers, as if they were visiting a patient. Once at the hospital, the receptionists, doctors, and nurses arranged for the refugees to be admitted as patients, giving them fictitious names and diagnoses, and assigning them to different hospital wards. Later, large groups of Jews were smuggled out of the hospital and taken to the coast and then to Sweden. Once, a funeral procession left a hospital with 200 Jews hidden in cars.[5]

A widow with six children housed and fed refugees and found fishermen who would take them across the water. At more than fifty points along the coast of Denmark, 300 boats—large fishing boats and small rowboats—made a total of a thousand crossings to Sweden, saving nearly 8,000 people, the majority of them Jewish.[6]

The Lutheran church was one of the most vocal demonstrators against the Nazis. While Jews were being rounded up by the Nazis, Lutheran church leaders read the following letter of protest at their Sunday services:

> We understand by freedom of religion the right to exercise our faith in God in such a way that race and religion can never in themselves be reason for depriving a man of his rights, freedom or property. Despite different religious views, we shall therefore struggle to ensure the continued guarantee to our Jewish brothers and sisters of the same freedom we ourselves treasure more than life itself.[7]

Thousands of normal citizens acted in heroic defense of their neighbors because of their experience of living well in a community of different religions and because of their profound belief in the humanity of all. "First a human—then a Christian."

In the end, only 500 Danish Jews were captured by the Nazis and sent to the concentration camp in Theresienstadt (where about 10 percent of them died). The majority of Danish Jews had escaped to safety in Sweden. At the end of the war, nearly 99 percent of the Danish Jews were still alive.

When the Danish Jews returned to their homes eighteen months after fleeing, many found their homes just as they had left them: none of their

4. Werner, *Conspiracy of Decency*, 51.

5. Werner, *Conspiracy of Decency*, 49.

6. Werner, *Conspiracy of Decency*, 61.

7. Werner, *Conspiracy of Decency*, 48. Cited in Yahil, *Rescue of Danish Jewry*, 235–36.

belongings had been stolen or damaged, their gardens had been tended to by their neighbors, and they found their apartments well-cleaned and maintained. Most of them were enthusiastically welcomed back by their neighbors.[8] (Contrast this with other European Jews who survived the Holocaust then returned to their homes to find them destroyed or belonging to someone else.)

In 1953 the Israeli parliament established a center to document and remember the Holocaust. It is called Yad Vashem—"a place to memorialize"—and one of the ways of remembering is honoring the rescuers by name and recounting their courageous deeds. These rescuers are called "The Righteous among the Nations." Despite the countless acts of bravery within Denmark, the list includes only twenty-two names from Denmark. A special note explains: "The Danish Underground requested that all its members who participated in the rescue of the Jewish community not be listed individually, but commemorated as one group."[9] This request beautifully reflects the solidarity of the people and their community. Together hundreds, if not thousands, of people acted with one mind-set—"first a human." They did not see their acts as heroic, just normal.

Emmy Werner, who researched the rescue of the Danish Jews, calls their communal acts "a conspiracy of decency." She writes,

> For many Danes the rescue of the Jews became a spontaneous act of protest against the German occupation. Doctors, nurses, taxi drivers, students, teachers, and fishermen alike joined the rescue efforts. The king, the bishops, the Supreme Court, the universities, Danish politicians and policemen, the trade unions, and professional and business organizations protested publicly and provided the leadership for many Danes from all walks of life who joined the rescue efforts.[10]

Today we need new "conspiracies of decency." Not a "conspiracy of heroic bravery" or a "conspiracy of unusual acts," just decency. It is decent to treat others as human, to treat them as we would treat ourselves. "First a human—then a Christian."

The Danish people, following the example of Jesus, compassionately stood up for their oppressed brothers and sisters. When a leper knelt at Jesus's feet begging for healing, Jesus was "moved with compassion" (Mark

8. Werner, *Conspiracy of Decency*, 5.

9. "Names of Righteous by Country," Yad Vashem.

10. Werner, *Conspiracy of Decency*, 170.

1:40–41 NASB). Jesus traveled to towns and villages, and "when he saw the crowds, he had compassion on them, because they were harassed and helpless, like sheep without a shepherd" (Matt 9:35–36 NIV).

Followers of Jesus should use their creative imagination and unique skills and resources in their own conspiracy of decency (and see how many of their friends they can enlist in this conspiracy!).

10

The Syrophoenician Woman

<hr>

Sometimes when I read the words of Jesus, I wonder if I'm the only one who thinks, "What the heck does that mean? He's not making any sense." Or, "Wow, that was rude." Like when he says to his mother at a wedding, "Woman, why do you involve me?" I'd never get away with calling my mother "woman"!

And what about that time he called that poor woman a bitch?

You don't remember that one? You probably don't even believe that Jesus could call someone a bitch. Here's the story.

> A Canaanite woman from [the region of Tyre and Sidon] came to him, crying out, "Lord, Son of David, have mercy on me! My daughter is demon-possessed and suffering terribly."
>
> Jesus did not answer a word. So his disciples came to him and urged him, "Send her away, for she keeps crying out after us."
>
> He answered, "I was sent only to the lost sheep of Israel."
>
> The woman came and knelt before him. "Lord, help me!" she said.
>
> He replied, "It is not right to take the children's bread and toss it to the dogs."
>
> "Yes it is, Lord," she said. "Even the dogs eat the crumbs that fall from their master's table." (Matt 15:22–27 NIV)

Did you catch that? Jesus refers to her as a dog, which, in its ancient context, would have been understood as something in the neighborhood of "bitch." In case you think he meant something else or was just joking, look at his other responses to her. His first response was to ignore her. When she approaches him respectfully with the words, "Lord, Son of David," and begs his mercy, he *ignores* her. When his disciples bug him about her, he seems to—pardon me—whine a little: "I was sent only to the lost sheep of Israel." In other words, "You're not on my team; I'm not responsible for you."

Is it just me or is Jesus being rude and dismissive?

This woman, though, is insistent—she falls to her knees, begging, "Lord, help me!" In his third response to her, Jesus insults her, calling her a dog, claiming that it wouldn't be right for him to help her because he's only responsible for his own.

What are we to do with this story of a Jesus who did not seem gentle, meek, or mild?

Let's look a little closer. Who was this woman? She is a Canaanite (also called a Phoenician). Jews considered the Canaanites to be doglike—rough, uncivilized, definitely not God's chosen (probably not even worthy of God's attention). And she is a woman, a second-class citizen, and a pagan. In the ancient context, she is unworthy of any respect. Finally, she gave birth to a demon-possessed child (you can hear the crowd grumbling: "Probably the mother's fault. I'd never raise a child like that."). Who wouldn't look down upon a woman who was a poor, pagan, Canaanite (dog) mother of a demon-possessed child?

Yet she's persistent and desperate. So she approaches Jesus to ask for his mercy on, of all things, her demon-possessed daughter. More grumbling from the crowd: "Little surprise there—after all, the poor girl was raised in *that* kind of society by *that* kind of a mother."

In reality, we know very little about the mother; the text doesn't tell us. I doubt the disciples knew much about her either. That's how prejudice works. They based their reactions on their prejudgment of *those* Phoenicians (and women, and pagans, and . . .) and then insisted that Jesus send her away.

Yet the woman throws herself in front of Jesus and begs, "Lord, help me."

At this point, a bone-weary Jesus flippantly sends her away with a rude comment. "It is not right to take the children's bread and toss it to the dogs." He's not just sending her away, he says that it would be wrong/unjust of him to help her.

The woman, though, is not budging. Truth is, she has nowhere else to go. Her daughter is possessed, she's a powerless woman, and she's a Canaanite, a despised race. In desperation she responds, "Even the dogs eat the crumbs that fall from their master's table."

This is how she sees her place in the world: she's a dog and she knows her place, but even dogs get to eat the crumbs. She has seen the bounty on other people's tables—food, shelter, clothes, warmth, and even respect—and she has waited patiently for their scraps. She's probably had scraps of men's affection, but no man would admit fathering a demon-possessed daughter. She's endured rude comments and mistreatment. She sees clearly how her culture works—how rich and powerful men call the shots, and how women and the poor and needy are beneath contempt. She has experienced firsthand the vicious, exclusionary side of humanity.

Her desperate act, then, is a profoundly unselfish love. For her daughter's sake, she dares to talk to a man, and a Jewish one at that. And she's asking him to brush just a few crumbs from his table to the ground for her to scavenge.

Jesus seems to restrict his love to the children of Israel. Perhaps this was his human, culturally conditioned side speaking. Her motivation was love for *her* child—"I love my daughter more than myself." She is willing to risk everything for the good of her daughter. But perhaps she has heard or seen enough of Jesus to take such a risk with hope.

While she might be considered and even treated like a dog in her earthly society, perhaps she hopes for something better in the kingdom of God. Perhaps she hopes that Jesus' kingdom extends beyond the borders of Israel, that his banquet is lavish enough that even its leftovers—even its crumbs—would suffice to heal her daughter. In that kingdom, her daughter wouldn't be denied healing compassion. Perhaps she hopes that divine love is not as carefully circumscribed as her nightmare life in this culture.

Finally Jesus agrees: "Then Jesus said to her, 'Woman, you have great faith! Your request is granted.' And her daughter was healed at that moment" (Matt 15:28 NIV).

This story is a puzzle. I don't know if Jesus learned at that moment that God's love was not restricted to the children of Israel. I don't know if this woman caused him to realize, for the first time, the pain of human prejudice and the powerlessness of outsiders. After all, he was born a baby and must have learned these things at some time (through some sort of experience). We don't tend to think of Jesus learning at all, and we mostly ignore that he was a human. As a human, he spoke a specific language, took on a specific culture's habits, and was inculcated in that culture's values. Perhaps he too, like us, needed to unlearn cultural prejudices and tribalism (our natural tendency to hang out with people like ourselves and to exclude the outsider—people who are different). Perhaps he had to learn that there is no circumscribing the love of God, that the borders of God's kingdom extend beyond Israel, and that even dogs (cultural outsiders and the dispossessed) get the crumbs off the table. Perhaps God used the Syrophoenician woman to teach Jesus to burst the bounds of finite, human, exclusionary love.

Perhaps. Regardless of how Jesus learned it, *we* can learn from this story that there are no bounds to the love of God. God does not restrict his love to the children of Israel, nor does he restrict his love to followers of Jesus. The Master's table is set for everyone.

Followers of Jesus, then, must extend their compassion to those outside of their community. We should beg crumbs for *someone else*—someone culturally "lesser" than ourselves—a homeless beggar, a hapless prisoner, a sick child, an atheist, or a Muslim. These people may be disvalued or looked down on by members of our community, but they have infinite value in the kingdom of God. They deserve compassion.

The lowly pagan woman with a demon-possessed child understood the kingdom of God in a deeper and fuller way than did the religious leaders of her day. She saw in Jesus a compassionate love that transcended cultural boundaries: he touched lepers, dined with tax collectors, and lived with the poor.

As followers of Christ, we, too, must burst the bounds of our own limited, prejudiced, and culturally circumscribed love. We must throw open the doors and invite all to come in.

11

Purveyors of Hate

On May 20, 2013, a tornado devastated Oklahoma City, killing eighteen people, including a number of small children, and injuring hundreds of others. As if the devastation weren't enough, some Christians, claiming to speak on behalf of God, added their hatred to the suffering. Just prior to the tornado, NBA player Jason Collins had come out as gay. Fred Phelps Jr., of the Westboro Baptist Church, blamed the tornado's death and destruction on Oklahoma City Thunder superstar Kevin Durant who had expressed his support for Collins. He tweeted, "OK Thunder's Durant flips God by praising fag Collins. God smashes OK. You do the math." Two minutes later, Phelps chimed in again: "God's wonderful wrath in Oklahoma reminds me: GodCursesUForFagMarriage. GodIsYourTerrorist."

Christians who claim to know the cause of human suffering outdo Jesus himself. When asked why the Tower of Siloam collapsed and killed eighteen people, Jesus humbly professed ignorance of the reason for the disaster (Luke 13:1–5). "Why did God make the tower fall on those people? Were they, of all the residents of Siloam, particularly evil? Tell us, what was their sin?" the crowd of people wanted to know. Jesus replied: "Do you think that these Galileans were worse sinners than all the other Galileans, because they suffered in this way?" Then Jesus befuddles those who proclaim themselves privy to the sins of those who are suffering. He instructs the questioners not to seek the sin of sufferer but to look within, into their own hearts.

Jesus subverts the desire to revel in divine payback (and, then, to feel good about our own righteousness because no towers have collapsed on us). The tower, he says, should warn us only of our own mortality and, hence, of our own need to get right with God. It should not occasion prideful reflection on the sins of others.

Even if we could be sure that the Oklahoma tornado were divine judgment, why would we not blame it on our own sins? For example, our lack of concern for the poor, the widow, or the oppressed? Why is it always someone else's sins that are to blame? Where Jesus used a disaster to focus on one's self, purveyors of hate use disasters to focus on the sins of others (and, as a consequence, to feel morally and spiritually superior about themselves).

You might be thinking that I'm picking low-hanging fruit by relying on the tweets of a kooky representative of the cult-like Westboro Baptist Church. Aren't there only forty-seven members of that church? You might say that I'm painting all Christians with the Westboro Baptist brush.

Let me be clear—I don't attribute Westboro Baptist's views to all Christians. In fact, I don't think their actions are Christian at all. Their views are the opinions of a few eccentric people who, while claiming some special understanding of God, violate the clear teachings of Jesus in both their words and their actions.

So why write about them? I picked Westboro Baptist because, although they profess fidelity to the teachings of Jesus and are popular with the media, they don't represent Christianity; in fact, such purveyors of hate are deeply unchristian.

The worst representatives of Christianity should not be taken as representative of Christianity. It's not fair. Simple as that.

Here's the flip-side: we have done to others precisely what we don't want done to us. We have taken the opinions of a minority of extremists as representative of Islam. And that's just plain not fair. When we do that, we are likely to have misunderstood Muhammad and his teachings because of extremist, selective caricatures of Islam. And that ain't right. We've judged all Muslims and even Islam itself based on the beliefs of the most extreme views of a very small minority of Muslims.

The events of 9/11 showed us the ugly face of a few extremists. But it did not show us the *heart* of Islam. Or the heart of the vast majority of Muslims.

What is the heart of Islam, true Islam?

Islam is defined, first and foremost, by its so-called Five Pillars, which include submission to God, prayer, giving to the poor and needy, fasting during the month of Ramadan, and pilgrimage to Mecca. That, pure and simple, is the heart of Islam.

Islam's first pillar—submission to the all-merciful and all-just God—is the perfect antidote to extremism. In the United States, regular mosque attendance is associated with an increase in civic and social engagement and a *decrease* in radicalism. Mosque attendance along with regular prayers reinforce belief in God's mercy and justice, motivating compassion towards one's neighbors and inoculating against extremist violence.

Indeed, extremist groups like ISIS and al Qaeda prey on religiously ignorant and socially alienated Muslims who are disconnected from their own communities; in their recruitment process, they discourage contact with local Muslims and inculcate their vicious and violent interpretation of "Islam." Isolation and inculcation are the keys to their success.

Let me relate submission to prayer. Most Muslims believe they should pray to God five times a day. Muslims—*five times a day*—bow and prostrate themselves in submission to God. In so doing, they ritually remind themselves—*five times a day*—that they are not God. There is one God, Allah, and it is not them. As an antidote to human pride, this ritual practice—*five times a day*—is a very good thing.

What about Islam's attitudes towards unbelievers?

It is useful to recall the opening lines of the Quran, which describe Allah as the most Merciful and Beneficent. Since mercy and compassion are the first and foremost attributes of God, mercy and compassion should be the first and foremost attributes of the followers of Allah, even in their relationships with non-believers.

The Quran rejects compulsion or coercion in matters of religion (2:256). It likewise asserts that while the Omnipotent could have made everyone believe in Allah ("a single people"), he permitted religious diversity so that everyone would freely strive for compassion and righteousness (5:48); one clear demonstration of compassion and righteousness, indicated by the context of the verse, is how well one treats strangers (those of different religious beliefs and practices). On the basis of these verses, the earliest followers of Prophet Muhammad forbade the mistreatment of Christians and Jews. For example, in the seventh century, Muslim leader Khalid ibn al-Walid, a companion of Muhammad, signed a treaty protecting Christians that said, "In the name of God, you have complete security for your churches which shall not be occupied by the Muslims or destroyed."[1] There is much more to be said on this matter, of course, but non-coercion and compassion constitute the heart of Islam toward non-believers.

None of us wants to believe that our religion is a religion of hate. But we have haters amongst us (Muslim and Christian alike). Still, the haters don't represent our religions. We should not judge Islam by the worst and least representative of its lot (just as we don't want Christianity to be judged by the worst of its lot). Just as Fred Phelps, Jr. of the Westboro Baptist Church does not speak for Christianity, so, too, a handful of radical Muslims do not speak for Islam. Just as the Westboro Baptist Church, bombers of abortion clinics, and the Ku Klux Klan do not represent Christianity, so, too, ISIS, the Taliban, and al Qaeda do not represent Islam.

The heart of Islam, like the heart of Christianity, is an all-merciful, all-just God. Deep faith in God, for both traditions, should motivate mercy and justice, not viciousness and violence.

1. Nye, "To Any Would-Be Terrorists."

12

Snap Judgments

———

L et me be honest. I am writing about our snap judgments of people who
are different from us—about our prejudices and fears—but I am not
above them. When I'm walking down the street in a "bad neighborhood"
and come upon a group of young black men in hoodies, my heart begins to
race, my eyes search for escape routes, my pace quickens. When I'm on an
airplane and a bearded, olive-skin man in a white robe stands up, I feel an
adrenaline surge, think about how to subdue him, and wonder if I'll survive
the crash. These fears and prejudices well up unsummoned.

I know that I, a white person, am vastly more likely to be attacked by
another white person, but I don't fear white people. More people are shot by
toddlers than killed by Muslims extremists, but I don't fear toddlers. And
while the vast majority of terrorist attacks on US soil are by non-Muslims,
I fear only Muslims.[1] I don't fear whites and toddlers and Christians. I fear
blacks and Arabs and Muslims—people who don't look like me.

Our instant fear of people who look different from us was a healthy
defense mechanism, protecting our own family and community from
threats to its survival. We're hardwired to quickly form judgments about
who's in and who's out of our families, tribes, and communities. Our ancestors who lived on the Serengeti faced fierce competition with other groups

1. Washington's Blog, "Non-Muslims Carried Out."

of people over scarce resources. Those who were capable of instantly identifying those who were within their own tribe and those who were not likely lived longer and so passed their tribe-identifying genes on to succeeding generations.

Snap judgments served our ancient ancestors well at a time when their lives were much more violent than ours. Pre-historians believe that throughout early human history, the likelihood of an adult male being killed in battle was about 65 percent—so much for the myth of the noble, peaceful savage. Fear drove them to develop a natural suspicion and distrust of those not in their group—those different from themselves.

Snap judgments of in-group/out-group are first and foremost based on looks—the color of skin or hair, the shape of the brow, or general body shape and size.[2] But, since early human groups probably didn't have physical features all that different from their nearest neighbors, clothing, tattoos, accents, face paint, and hairdos figured in as well. Even the way members of different groups smell factors into identifying in-group or out-group. We like the way those within our own group smell, and dislike the ways members of other groups smell.

In-group/out-group judgments are likewise good/bad judgments.[3] In-group is good: family, friend, neighbor, sharer of the same values and worshipper of the true god. Out-group is bad: competitor, enemy, stranger, evil, and worshipper of idols. We make moral judgments based on the "funny" smell of members of other groups.[4] Everyone smells, but those outside our tribe *stink*.

In-group, good; out-group, bad. Got it.

Here's another way to put it—everyone is a racist (or a bigot).

In January 2015, extremists killed twelve people at the offices of the French satirical newspaper *Charlie Hebdo*. The phrase *Je Suis Charlie* ("I am Charlie") swept Twitter and then Facebook and then newspapers and then the world. *Je Suis Charlie* expressed empathy for the cartoonists as well as support for freedom of speech. Millions of people, including more than forty world leaders, marched the streets of Paris in solidarity. These world leaders included British Prime Minister David Cameron, German Chancellor Angela Merkel, Israeli Prime Minister Benjamin Netanyahu, Palestinian President Mahmoud Abbas, Malian President Ibrahim Boubacar Keita,

2. Ojiaku, "Is Everybody a Racist?"

3. Avenanti et al., "Racial Bias."

4. "Smell Report," Social Issues Research Center (website).

EU President Donald Tusk, and Jordan's King Abdullah II. In March 2016, thirty-five people were killed by extremists in a Brussels train station. The world and world leaders again rallied in support, signs of *Je Suis Bruxelles* made every major newspaper.

At about the same time, Turkey experienced a series of bomb blasts that killed and injured vastly more than the *Charlie Hebdo* attack. Over 150 innocent people were killed, and over 500 innocent people were injured. But we are not Turkey, and the world's silence was as deafening as its support for *Charlie Hebdo* and Brussels.[5] No one was talking about the Turkey massacres, no one was protesting the deaths of Turkey's innocents, and no world leaders officials marched in Turkey's streets in solidarity.

Why were so many *Charlie Hebdo* but so few Turkey?

We were *Charlie Hebdo* because the French are a lot like us (good)— white, upper-middle class, Western, European, Christian, enlightened, liberal. We were not Turkey because they are very different from us (bad)— brown, lower class, Middle Eastern, Arab, Muslim, medieval, backward, and retrograde (most of this is mistaken, but when making snap judgments, one needn't trouble oneself with the facts). If we were to actually visit Turkey, we'd probably think that Turks stink.

In the week that followed Brussels, extremists killed four times as many non-Westerners (Muslims) as Westerners (non-Muslims). On March 25, suicide bombers attacked a soccer stadium in Baghdad, killing forty-one and wounding over a hundred.[6] That same day, at least twenty-six people were murdered in a triple suicide bombing in Aden, Yemen.[7] On March 27, the Taliban detonated a bomb in Lahore, Pakistan, killing more than seventy people and wounding over three hundred.[8] Yet Baghdad, Aden, and Lahore slipped our notice.

I may be Brussels but I am not Baghdad, Aden, or Lahore. I am not Baghdad, Aden, or Lahore because I am white, Western, Christian (good) and they are not (bad).

We not only fear those who are different from us, we lack sympathy for them when they suffer. Study after study shows a measurable decrease

---

5. Rice, "There's a Massive Double Standard."
6. Salim and Sly, "Islamic State Suicide Bomber."
7. "Yemen Suicide Bomb."
8. Fenton, "Lahore Blast."

in empathetic brain responses to the pain of people of other races and in other groups.[9]

Such fears and failures to sympathize, though normal and natural, are failures of love. Fear and the divisiveness and even violence it creates define the kingdom of this world. But Jesus' kingdom is not of this world. In Jesus' kingdom, fear will be overwhelmed by love. The world is a frightening place, so we developed fear-based defense mechanisms to help us survive against those who are not our kin or in our tribe. Ignoring but then conceding to our fears in this day and age leads to suspicion, anger, hatred, prejudice, violence, and war. Each step toward love, though, is a step away from fear.

In 1 John 4:18 we read, "There is no fear in love. But perfect love drives out fear." Learning to love is the way of unlearning fear.

I don't know how to love in general. God may have so loved the entire world, but I don't. We love people, particular people, one at a time. Learning to love people who are different from us requires overcoming fears and suspicions and takes time to get to know and then to respect and even honor just one person at a time. Swallow your fears and find a particular person and initiate a relationship. It might be your neighbor. You might have to visit a mosque or a temple or synagogue. But take your first tiny step toward expanding the kingdom of God, one love-overcoming-fear step at a time.

9. Ojiaku, "Is Everybody a Racist?"

13

Joel's Stein

———

Ihave a friend, let's call him Joel, who collects junk—Joel the Junk Collector. At least once or twice a week, Joel visits secondhand stores and scours the shelves. He has a keen eye for junk. While foraging one day, a flashy German stein caught Joel's eye. But he was carrying no cash. So he asked the clerk to set it aside until he returned the next day. Upon his return, Joel spied a patron examining his treasured stein and Joel demanded its return; the patron refused. Joel prevailed upon the clerk, reminding him of his promise to hold the stein for him until his return. The clerk intervened, grabbed the gaudy stein from the hands of the other patron, and returned it to Joel. Joel paid five dollars and, beaming proudly, departed with his prize.

On arriving home, Joel's exasperated wife sighed at the addition of one more thing to his ever-growing pile of junk. Joel's basement, you see, is completely clogged and cluttered with his accumulating treasures.

A couple of years later, Joel, in need of cash to pay for his daughter's college tuition, listed his stein on eBay. He brushed aside his wife's scoffing; she was certain that no one would pay much of anything for that worthless piece of trash. Hardly worth the time. Definitely not worth the space it had taken up.

To his wife's surprise, the bidding for the stein was fast and furious. Joel's five-dollar bargain sold on eBay for $850. The stein, it turns out, was no worthless piece of junk. It was a highly valued and rare treasure for which people were willing to pay handsomely (which, of course, Joel knew all along).

The value of the stein was not evident by just looking at it. It was, as my mother would say when she didn't like something, "different." It seemed too big, bulky even, and over-decorated, gaudy. And it was, in the end, just a glazed hunk of clay.

But Joel knew what his wife didn't—the stein's value didn't depend on its earthy ingredients and humble origins; its value depended entirely on people's esteem for it. The more people esteemed it, the higher its price would be. The stein was worth whatever anyone was willing to pay for it.

You might think that humans, who were created from dust and to dust they will return, are of little consequence. Humanity's earthy ingredients and humble origins, after all, don't exactly suggest great value. A few years ago, I read an article which estimated that the chemicals in the human body are worth about five dollars. We're water, mostly, but we're also made up of carbon, nitrogen, calcium, phosphorous, sulfur (that explains a lot!), and magnesium, with a pinch of lithium, strontium, and vanadium. Taking inflation into account, maybe we're worth about seven dollars now.

That's all on the plus side. Shouldn't we also subtract from our value the shameful things humans do? Human selfishness and ignorance continually seek new opportunities for expression. Starting with seven dollars and subtracting our moral failings, it's hard to conceive of humans as worth all that much.

The Bible seems to concur on these points. Based just on our chemical makeup and wickedness, we seem worthless. In Psalm 8:4, the psalmist asks of God: "What is [hu]mankind that you are mindful of them? Human beings that you care for them?" (NIV) Who are we, piddly humans, that God should care for us? We are vessels of clay in more or less gaudy dress.

The psalmist doesn't end there and neither does our value. Our worth, like the stein's, comes from another's esteem for us, another's valuing of us. In our case, we are esteemed and valued by God. The psalmist puts it this way: God has made us just a bit lower than the angels and crowned us with glory and honor.

We are much more than clay in an attractive (or not) package. According to the psalm we bear glory and honor not because we are inherently glorious or worthy of honor. We are valuable because of the unexpected, unmerited, and incalculable esteem in which God holds us. Here's how we are valued: God esteems us and so we are worth an infinite amount. Just as Joel has an eye for steins, God has an eye for us.

The value of a stein goes up and down based on supply and demand. The more steins there are, the less each one is worth. And if no one wants a stein, its value declines to zero.

Here's the difference between us and steins (okay, this is one, among many others; for example, steins are good at holding beer, while not all humans are): our value never decreases. Because our price is fixed by God's unwavering desire for each and every one of us, we are always infinitely valuable. This is no monopoly, no price-fixing conspiracy; this is just how the divine economy works. God desires us infinitely; therefore we are infinitely valued and valuable.

Even though the world is crawling with an abundance of human creatures (excessive supply), God values each and every one of us infinitely (incredible demand).

So our value does not go up and down depending on the demand for carbon or how we look or how much we earn or how other human beings desire us. Our value is fixed once and for all by God's unwavering and infinite esteem for us.

According to the Bible, we are doubly valued. We have infinite worth both as bearers of God's image and as recipient's of God's infinite esteem. Either way—as image-bearers of an infinite God or as infinitely esteemed by God—we get the same result. We are, each and every one of us, infinitely valuable.

What about human attitudes towards human beings?

The biblical view is that we should value what God values and love as God loves. Since God unwaveringly values each and every human being, *we* should value each and every human being. Since God does not value persons based on their looks or wealth or nationality or social class, *we* should not value persons based on their looks or wealth or nationality or social class.

It's just plain wrong for us to diminish what God has declared valuable.

But by not valuing other persons as God values, we are not likely to love other persons as God loves. Our diminishment of other human beings—based as it so often is on skin color, social class, gender, nationality, religion, etc.—can lead, if unchecked, from put-downs to intolerance to violence.

As hard and scary as it is, we need to value other humans as God does and then to love other humans as God does. Following God, we need to "crown every person with glory and honor."

14

Pharisees and Publicans

Our self-worth, to summarize much of what has gone before, is based on comparisons. If I can divide the world into groups, and ascribe superiority to my group, I can then establish my self-worth and ultimate significance. In other words, I diminish the world to expand myself. We all do this. For example, men divide the world in half, preferring the male gender to that of the other—"I'm glad that I was born a man." Entire cultures eliminate female contenders from the race for glory by preventing their participation in the workforce, civic life, the arts and sciences, or even the marketplace. That infant girls can be regularly discarded at birth in some cultures indicates the lack of value attributed to them. By eliminating better than 50 percent of the people in the world from the competition, my race is half won.

We also believe that our own social-cultural heritage is intrinsically preferable to that of others, not simply different from but better than others in a moral and even spiritual sense. American ethnocentrism is appealing because it seeks to accord us a status above peoples of other cultures. "I'm proud to be an American" is often more than simply a slogan proclaiming one's patriotism; it also betrays a judgment of the secondary status of people living in "lesser" societies. The terms we use to describe other cultures are heavily value-laden and tilt the scales in favor of our own culture. We call other sociocultural groups foreign, backward, primitive, savage, commie, pagan, uncivilized, old-fashioned, fundamentalist, third-world, or developing. Those skilled in the process of cultural derision can eliminate virtually every other culture from the race for glory.

There is a deep human need to feel superior. To do so we must tell ourselves these stories which ascribe to us self-worth at the expense of others. Our lives are filled with artificial conventions designed to increase our perceived self-worth: we try to please others, to get ahead, to gain power, to be recognized, and to stand out, all for the sake of our egos. We are social creatures because we need to munch on others to feed our starving egos.

One day, Jesus also told a story about egos:

> Two men went up to the temple to pray, one a Pharisee and the other a tax collector. The Pharisee stood by himself and prayed: "God, I thank you that I am not like other people—robbers, evil-doers, adulterers—or even like this tax collector. I fast twice a week and give a tenth of all I get."
>
> But the tax collector stood at a distance. He would not even look up to heaven, but beat his breast and said, "God, have mercy on me, a sinner."
>
> I tell you that this man, rather than the other, went home justified before God. For all those who exalt themselves will be humbled, and those who humble themselves will be exalted. (Luke 18:10–14 NIV)

Those listening to Jesus knew exactly what the labels *Pharisee* and *tax collector* meant. If you were a Pharisee, everyone knew you were at the top of the religious heap: you were in a position of spiritual authority, you were zealous about the Jewish law, you kept all the rules, you fasted regularly, and you were definitely right with God. If you were a tax collector, everyone knew you were at the very bottom: you were greedy, you were a thief, you preyed on those who worked hard, you made your living off of other people's money, and you were most definitely *not* right with God.

The way Jesus ended his story—"I tell you that this man, rather than the other, went home justified before God"—was a surprise to these people. The tax collector was justified before God? The Pharisee wasn't? That's not right. That's not how the world works.

Who exactly was Jesus speaking to that day? The text in Luke tells us: "To some who were confident of their own righteousness and looked down on everyone else, Jesus told this parable" (Luke 18:9 NIV).

Let's consider that introduction again: *To some who were confident of their own righteousness and looked down on everyone else, Jesus told this parable.*

This means that Jesus was probably speaking to actual Pharisees. His audience was probably men, probably wealthy men, and probably wealthy men who held leadership positions. We know the audience members were confident in their own rightness before God and that "they looked down on everyone else." They perceived themselves to be superior to others (and according to society's pecking order, the Pharisees *were* above others). Look at the Pharisee, standing before God, reminding God of his worthiness: "I pray, I fast, I tithe." Jesus says, not in so many words, "This man has 'I' trouble."

By putting this introduction with this parable, Luke seems to be saying that these types of things go together: religious confidence, arrogance, and self-righteousness. That is, when I am confident of my own rightness before God, then I naturally assume those who are different from me must not be right before God. When I elevate myself, I diminish others.

How confident are you of your own righteousness? Of your faith? Jesus says to you, "Be humble. Don't look down on people who are different from you; don't assume that they can't be right before God. And don't be deluded about yourself. Don't assume that because you keep all the rules you are justified before God." Just because you fast, pray, and obey all the rules doesn't mean you're top dog in God's kingdom. If you look down on someone for their beliefs and practices (the Muslim fundamentalist, say, or the Jewish teenager, or the atheist "infidel"), thus feeling superior in any way, you become the Pharisee.

Your response to God, then, should be to fall humbly on your knees, look only to God for your righteousness, and say, with the publican, "God, have mercy on me, a sinner."

15

Angels Unawares

Christians know they should love their brothers and sisters in Christ, but what should their attitude be toward non-Christians, toward people they believe have denied God's truth? Christians, after all, believe that the only way to God is through Jesus. In their defense of God, some Christians have proven as zealous as the most radical extremists of other religions.

I have heard some Christians say that Muslims worship a different (false) God; therefore they are idolators who warrant loathing and contempt, not respect and compassion. Some Christians say that Jews, often viewed as the crucifiers of Jesus, are either hypocritical Pharisees ("whitewashed tombs—beautiful on the outside but full of dead men's bones and uncleanness on the inside") or self-righteous Sadducees (a "brood of vipers"). Although they were once God's chosen people, the Jews rejected the gospel, so God offered it to the gentiles. (Interestingly, Jews and Israel are viewed considerably more favorably than Muslims because of the positive role Christians believe Jews play in the end-times.) Although Christian antisemitism is both shameful and lamentable, it seems to follow a perverse logic from these shameful and lamentable beliefs about Jews.

Back to our question. How can you love someone whose religious beliefs are so fundamentally opposed to your own? More pointedly: How can you love someone who fails, according to your deepest beliefs, to honor

God? God is to be loved in spirit and truth, and the truth about God is that Jesus is the visible image of the invisible God. Those who don't bow their knee to Jesus are not worshipping the one, true God. How can you love or even respect someone who, according to your Christian beliefs, dishonors God?

Let's start with respect, and work our way up to love.

Many years ago, an overweight, unattractive, cognitively impaired, and unemployed, middle-aged man (I'll call him Fred), showed up at my apartment on a Saturday evening at 8 o'clock. Fred was a prominent local indigent who made regular rounds to churches and even to the homes of some church members (after following them home). Some people were scared and others just displeased when Fred arrived at their door. He seldom showered, he talked incessantly about his gloomy life, and he was oblivious to normal social cues—especially the countless unsubtle cues telling him that it was time to go. I lived in an apartment with three other college students, and none of us wanted to spend our Saturday evenings hanging out with Fred. Honestly, anyone but Fred.

When I tried to put him off, saying that we were just about to leave, Fred burst into tears. He told me that he had already been to several homes that night, and no one was willing to spend time with him. Desperately lonely and at the end of his rope, he cried out: "I thought you Christians were supposed to love everyone!"

My roommate, Kirk, invited Fred in, canceled his plans to go out with us, and spent the evening sharing a meal and talking with Fred, the first of many days and nights that Kirk spent with Fred.

When I asked Kirk why he did it, he told me about a Bible verse: "Do not neglect to show hospitality to strangers, for thereby some have entertained angels unawares" (Heb 13:2 ESV).

Kirk gave me a new way of thinking about Fred. Fred was not just a large mound of smelly, in-the-way flesh. Fred was not just another annoyance. Maybe Fred was much, much more—maybe an angel. Maybe Kirk was right when he claimed to be entertaining an angel "unawares." Maybe not. Probably not. Fred was most likely just Fred.

But just Fred, I was beginning to learn, was enough.

Underneath Fred's socially unacceptable garb Kirk could see what I could not—angel wings. Or, with less theological baggage, Kirk could see Fred's deep and abiding and essential humanity. As such, Fred, like every other human being, deserved respect. Honor, even. And, as when any human being in need knocks on your door, hospitality. He deserved this just by virtue of being Fred, a human being.

Recall one of Abraham's curious encounters with God. In Genesis 18, we read that Abraham was relaxing inside his tent, avoiding the noonday sun. He glanced out and saw three strange men approaching. He ran out to them, bowed before them, and offered them a meal. As they were eating, the Lord (one of the three men) spoke to Abraham. No mere angel, Abraham was entertaining God unawares!

If Abraham had not shown hospitality to those strangers, he may have missed out on a life-changing encounter with God. But Abraham did what he was supposed to do—he saw three hungry strangers and invited them into his tent. He shared a meal and his life, and, lo and behold, one of them just happened to be the Lord. If he had let his fear of strangers overcome his sense of hospitality, he would have disrespected God himself. Abraham, it must be noted, had every reason to fear those strangers and little reason to show them hospitality. In his day and age, he was more likely to be robbed than rewarded by wayfaring strangers.

Yet Abraham invited in and shared a meal with three strange men, and the Lord began speaking to him.

Perhaps you're thinking, Fred was no angel, and he was certainly not God. And even if Fred were an angel, most strangers are not. Great stories, you're thinking, but how do they apply to our contemporary attitudes towards Muslims and Jews, you know, towards idolaters and murderers of the Christ?

Our fears say, "Build that wall," don't open the door.

The Christian view, however, is that stranger and neighbor alike deserve respect—respect of the sort that ushers in honor and hospitality. Honor and hospitality of the tear-down-the-wall and open-the-door variety.

Why should Christians respect and honor Muslims and Jews? While the religious "stranger" may not be an angel or God, the Bible is clear—they *are* icons of God. Humans are created in God's image (Gen 1:27) and so are god-*like*. Humans are not gods, but they mirror God. Therefore each and every person in the world reflects divine value. God's glory shines through and so ennobles each and every human being. By virtue of being an icon of God, each human is worthy of respect, honor, and hospitality. (There are other reasons, too, but this is the deepest reason.)

You can't reject an icon of God without rejecting God himself. If we let our fear of strangers overcome our sense of hospitality, we disrespect God himself.

I am required to show mercy because each person I meet is not just a hunk of flesh and blood, never a mere annoyance—each person is an angel unawares or an icon of God. As angel or icon, all persons are 100 percent worthy of respect and honor.

And of love. Although 1 Corinthians 13 is often read at weddings, St. Paul's model of love is not restricted to husband and wife. Love, St. Paul thinks, is the chief virtue, and the kingdom of God is marked by this fear-overcoming, humanity-honoring, and community-expanding sort of love.

> Love is patient, love is kind. It does not envy, it does not boast, it is not proud. It does not dishonor others, it is not self-seeking, it is not easily angered, it keeps no record of wrongs. Love does not delight in evil but rejoices with the truth. It always protects, always trusts, always hopes, always perseveres. (1 Cor 13:4–7 NIV)

Our lack of compassion toward Muslims and Jews is easily angered (engendering separation and even hostility). And it keeps a record of wrongs (often judging all Muslims by the extremist actions of a very few). Love, however, does not dishonor, is not easily angered, and keeps no record of wrongs.

When a stranger or a Fred walks by, then, our initial response should be hospitality. Reach out to them, invite them into our tent, and offer them a meal and ourselves. In so doing, we open ourselves to the God-transforming experience that changed Abraham's life.

16

What I've Learned from My Muslim and Jewish Friends

On my first trip to Turkey, I was generously invited into the home of a Muslim family for dinner. I was part of a group of Americans, and none of us knew our hosts. Nonetheless, our hosts were eager to share their food, their family, and their culture with nine strangers. The kindness of strangers would repeatedly surprise me in Turkey.

I was less surprised on later trips to Muslim-majority countries because on every trip in every country from Indonesia to Iran, Muslim strangers shared meals with me. I recall my first night visiting my daughter in Amman, Jordan. She took me to her favorite Yemeni restaurant which, a local favorite, was jam-packed. Not an empty table in the house. Two smiling men on the other side of the room enthusiastically waved us over. We fought our way through the crowded restaurant, and they gestured for us to sit down at the two empty seats at their table. We politely refused, but they just as politely insisted, with their hands and their smiles. Although my daughter spoke only broken Arabic and they spoke no English, they helped us order, let us know how delighted they were that we had joined them, and shared their already-delivered food. We ate and "talked" and laughed; we took a few selfies and shared them on Facebook and Snapchat. When we went to pay our bill, the restaurant manager informed us that it had been paid for by our Yemeni friends. They rebuffed our efforts to repay them and smiled widely as we said our good-byes.

But I write not to praise Muslim hospitality to strangers (which is eminently worthy of praise).

During that family dinner on my first trip to Turkey, one of our hosts excused himself. He was a local imam and went off to chant the evening's call to prayer over the loudspeakers. A few minutes later, we heard his familiar voice in lilting Arabic summoning the Turkish Muslim community to one of their five daily prayers. Other than noting that we could now hear our former host from afar, nothing remarkable happened. Our Muslim hosts did not leave the table en masse and walk to a nearby mosque to fulfill their obligation. One did leave the table for a while but quietly returned a few minutes later. I assumed she had been heating up some food or starting the coffee pot. Another left shortly thereafter, again returning with little notice a few minutes later. When a third got up to leave, I asked where everyone was going. They told me they were going to pray and said they would show me their prayer room later.

After dinner, they showed us the prayer room in their house with a prayer rug in the middle facing Mecca. Without calling any attention to themselves, they had slipped virtually unnoticed into this very private room, closed the door, and bowed down to pray to God. When I asked what they prayed, I was told that most prayers include the ritual incantation of

> There is no God but You
> In the Name of Allah, the Most Compassionate, the Most Merciful.
> Praise be to Allah, Lord of the Universe,
> the Most Compassionate, the Most Merciful!
> Master of the Day for Judgment!
> You alone do we worship and You alone do we call on for help.
> Guide us along the Straight Path.

In a prostrate position, with head touching the ground, five times a day, Muslims pray to the One, All-Merciful God to guide them along God's path.

I grew up in the Protestant Christian tradition, which emphasizes divine grace and denounces human "works" of righteousness. Rituals, we had been taught, were empty. We thought the attitude of our heart was more important than the position of our body. And grace alone demanded a trust in God's mercy we thought was absent from, say, Catholics and Muslims. I remember the first time I visited a Roman Catholic Church—I found kneeling down strange and even spiritually offensive. Although I've come a long way from my fundamentalist-Protestant, anti-Catholic roots, I was emotionally prepared to dislike the Muslim's ritual prostration and prayer.

But I didn't. My Muslim friends, I learned, were more concerned with a faithful heart than a prostrate body. And they likewise trusted more in God's abundant mercy than in their puny prayers. And I appreciated that ritually connecting to the All-Merciful was a really good thing. Finally, in their repeated recitations of "There is no God but You," I began to hear the radically unselfing and morally and spiritually fundamental truth, "I am not God."

I began to think that just about everyone—from fundamentalist Christian to devout atheist—could profit from bowing down five times a day to remind themselves that they are not God. We all need to be constantly decentered, constantly reminded that we are not the center of the universe, that the universe does not revolve around us. Coming to grips with the sober fact that we are not first in the cosmos makes it easier to treat others with respect. In fact, coming to grips with the fact that we are not God is a prerequisite to becoming, like God, merciful.

So I have learned from my Muslim friends the value of uncomfortable but unselfing rituals that remind us that we are not God, creating psychological and spiritual space for the kind of mercy that fearlessly reaches out even to the stranger.

And that's good.

On my first trip to Israel, I was invited to share the Sabbath with my coauthors, rabbis Arik Ascherman and Einat Ramon (contributors to my *Abraham's Children: Liberty and Tolerance in an Age of Religious Conflict*).

Arik, at the time, was executive director of Rabbis for Human Rights (RHR), a prominent Israeli human rights organization dedicated to protecting the rights of all Israelis. RHR is probably best known for its volunteers who served as human shields between settlers and the olive trees of Palestinian farmers. RHR was awarded the Niwano Peace Prize in 2006 and Arik, along with Rabbi Ehud Bandel, a cofounder of RHR, was awarded the Ghandi Peace Prize. Arik has been stoned, stabbed, beaten, and arrested for his peace and justice work. He attributes his peace work to the rabbinic concept of *tikkun olam* (acts of kindness aimed at, literally, "repairing the world").

Einat, Arik's wife, was the first Israeli-born woman to be ordained as a rabbi and the first woman to head a conservative rabbinical school. In addition to teaching Jewish thought and Jewish feminism at the Shechter Institute, she is a pioneer in Israel's clinical pastoral care movement, setting up the first clinical pastoral education unit in Israel.

But while Arik and Einat are both personally and professionally accomplished, that's not what I learned from my Jewish friends.

When Arik and Einat opened their doors on that Sabbath, they opened more than doors to their home; they opened their hearts to us (me and my two videographers, Geert Heetebrij and Phil Oosterhouse), and they opened my mind to their profound and mysterious relationship with God. From the smell of the food to the arrangement of the table to the lighting of the candles to the incantations in Hebrew, their religious world was, for lack of a better term, foreign (to me); I had neither the language nor the concepts to grasp or process what I was experiencing. I knew they were being faithful to the Fourth Commandment, to remember the Sabbath day and keep it holy. But that's about all I knew.

I didn't know why they refused to drive (or to be driven in a car), to turn on or off electric lights (so as not to kindle or extinguish a fire?), or to purchase the loaf of bread that Arik had forgotten to purchase earlier in the day. And my ADD body couldn't imagine how they could just sit for twenty-four hours and rest. At the time, I had no idea what Sabbath meant to them.

So I asked.

They explained that for six days one can work, but none is permitted on the seventh because "in six days the Lord made heaven and earth, the sea, and all that is in them, but rested the seventh day; therefore the Lord blessed the sabbath day and consecrated it" (Exodus 20:11 NRSV). Arik and Einat then explained the connection between the Sabbath and divine creation. Taking a break from acts of creation (work) and focusing one's entire attention on God is a weekly reminder that God is the creator of heaven and earth and all they contain. And, you are not. Every seventh day, amidst the hustle and bustle of one's very important (self-important) life, you must stop, cease, rest, and remember that you are not God.

Shabbat has other meanings, of course. And it means different things to different people. But this is what I learned from my Jewish friends, Arik and Einat: There is exactly one God. And it's not you.

And that's good.

Nancy Fuchs Kreimer

1

Sarah and Hagar

On my first day of Hebrew School, I fell in love with the Torah. Encountering my first Bible stories at the age of nine, I knew I had found a new home, my chosen "other world" in which to seek meaning. Although I grew up in a mostly secular setting, early on I had an intuition that life was more mysterious than anyone around me was letting on. The men and women in the Torah seemed to know something about that missing dimension for which I yearned. They called it God. I wanted to know more. And I still do.

Even on a strictly human level, those biblical characters fascinated me. Out of all the characters in all those stories, my favorite was Sarah. Here was a devoted wife who followed her husband, Abraham, into the unknown, devised a plan for him to have a child through her servant Hagar and, once becoming a mother herself, ensured a legacy for *her* son, Isaac. I wanted nothing more than what my idealized Sarah appeared to want: a good husband with a blessed future, and—of course—children! (Remember, this was the 1950s.)

For his part, Abraham was the very exemplar of faith. Moved only by a call from an unseen God, he left his family home and ventured to "a land that God would show him" (Gen 12). Together, this couple represented all that was good about our tradition: courage, a willingness to journey to new adventures, and a fierce desire to preserve Jewish identity into the next generation. Abraham was the activist who heard the call and responded; Sarah was the loyal wife who supported his every step. (Abraham's complicated story is a subject for another chapter. For now, we will focus on Sarah.)

Around the time I began college, the feminist movement awakened my generation to the limits of our dreams and the limitations of our role models. I went through a period when I did not think much of our Mother Sarah. (Nor was I impressed with my own mother who, considering her time and place, was actually a strong role model.) In the early days of feminism, coinciding with my late adolescence, humility was not in great supply.

Over the years, as my vision of humanity broadened, our matriarch Sarah continued to look worse and worse. I will never forget the day a rabbi began her sermon by saying, "Abraham did what his wife asked him to do: He raped her slave." Although that sounds harsh, the text of the Torah allows for that interpretation. After all, what do we call it when a master sleeps with a slave? Then Sarah asks Abraham to dismiss Hagar, knowing that in the wilderness, Hagar and her son, Ishmael, may die of thirst. Abraham sends them out, and Ishmael almost dies.

Like so much of the Torah, this story seems to beg for more—as if perhaps some crucial pieces of information have been omitted. Devoted readers of the text are left to construct those missing pieces out of their imaginations. They find secrets hidden in the gaps and the repetitions, in the connections between one passage and another, in what the Jerusalem Talmud calls the "white fire" in contrast to the letters written in "black fire" (Yerushalmi Shelamim 6:1, 49d).

That process of creative interpretation—of explicating the "white fire"—is known in Jewish tradition as midrash (literally, "to seek out"), and it began even before the Bible was complete. Christians will recognize some passages of the New Testament that are best read as midrashim (plural for midrash) on a Hebrew Bible text.[1] Today, when Jews read Torah, they often read it through the lens of the classical rabbinic midrashic tradition dating from 200 to 1200, especially as compiled by the eleventh-century scholar Rashi. Indeed, that first Torah story, which so compelled me—a tale of how Abraham reasoned his way to God—was actually a midrash. It was not in the Torah text itself.[2] And the process never really ended. Throughout his-

---

1. See Levine and Brettler, *Jewish Annotated New Testament.*

2. That particular midrash has parallels across other traditions. See Flusser, "Abraham and the Upanishads."

tory, Jews have been determined to discover the stories we need within the stories we have.

Much of Jewish tradition chooses to ignore or excuse Sarah's behavior, seeing it as a part of God's plan that the inheritance of Abraham's promise pass to Sarah's son, Isaac. But even early on, some readers were troubled. At least one traditional midrash has Hagar returning, in the guise of a woman named Keturah, to marry Abraham after Sarah's death. A great medieval commentator, Ramban (also called Nachmanides), was able to look this story in the eye and conclude that it had an ethical problem. He then redeemed the troubling text by speculating that the Jewish people's enslavement in Egypt (many generations later) was punishment precisely for the treatment of the Egyptian slave Hagar.

Still, the bulk of traditional Judaism sees Sarah as our beloved tribal mother and Hagar as the stranger, the "other woman." Jews and Muslims alike traditionally understand Hagar to be the mother of the Arab people and, by extension, all Muslims. How surprising, then, to come to synagogue services each year on the first day of Rosh Hashana, the Jewish New Year—with "standing room only" crowds—and discover that the star of the show is Hagar! The Torah reading that tradition calls for on that day is Genesis 21. The woman Sarah tried to banish from the story is back. And what a great character she is! Despite her unprivileged place as a woman, a foreigner, a slave, a single mother, Hagar is one strong, powerful woman. Indeed, she is the only person in the Torah—male or female—to dare to give a name to God (Gen 16:13).

Here we are, centuries later, with Jews and Arabs in conflict, Isaac and Ishmael still in dispute over who is Abraham's legitimate heir, who has the right to the land. On our holy day we are asked to grapple with the account of how the ancestral family first came apart. As you can imagine, there is no shortage of contemporary midrashim on this subject.

Some Jewish poets and preachers have taken this ambiguous Bible story and retold it in ways that speak to our hopes. They recognize that Sarah can hardly be blamed for the patriarchal society in which she lived, one that set her up as Hagar's adversary. Some imagine scenes the Bible does not include. Jewish singer-songwriter Linda Hirschhorn adapted a poem by Rabbi Lynn Gottlieb in which Sarah calls out to Hagar:

> Yes, I am your Sarah, I remember you, Hagar.
> Your voice cuts through the distance, no, you can't be very far.
> It was I who cast you out, in fear and jealousy;

Yet your vision survived the wilderness to reach your destiny.

But it wasn't till my Isaac lay under the knife
that I recognized your peril, the danger to your life.
I tremble now, O Hagar, for our peril's still the same:
We will not survive our danger till we speak each other's names.[3]

Between 2007 and 2016, I organized five retreats for Jewish and Muslim emerging religious leaders. The fourth retreat was for women only. With one less difference to negotiate, we hoped to see the rapid bonding that often happens in same-gender groups. We invited two women scholars to lead us in our shared passion for text study. The texts they chose were the stories of Sarah and Hagar in our respective Scriptures and interpretations. We looked forward to a time of intimacy and sharing.

Instead, it turned out to be the most difficult of the five retreats. Despite, or perhaps because of, our connection as women, other differences emerged more powerfully. Tensions churned under the surface and sometimes above. We noticed divisions that are often blurred at interfaith gatherings by our focus on religion. As race and class issues arose, the figures of Hagar and Sarah continued to haunt us. (Hagar's story of the strong, single slave mother has resonated with African Americans for centuries.) Sarah and Hagar did not necessarily help us find a way through the difficult conversations. In fact, what helped was a morning in which a Muslim participant allowed us to join in the traditional Sufi practice of chanting *Zikhr*, touching a spiritual chord that transcended our complicated intellects.

We sought the help of poetry. We found it in the work of my friend Mohja Kahf, a professor of literature who had written a poem that spoke to our longing. She later published that poem in a book, *Hagar Poems*, in which she explores the complexity of the relationship between these two iconic women, imperfect characters in an imperfect world.

Mohja's poem is an extended midrash on the dysfunctional family we share. Mohja constructs a future family reunion "out of the blue infinitude" that redeems Sarah, Hagar, and even Abraham. Together, they "dismantle the house of fear, brick by back-breaking brick." After Hagar's twelve grandchildren "pick up Sarah's twelve at the airport," the reunion turns to the pain the relatives share:

Sorrows furrow every face.
This, in the firelight, no one denies.

3. Hirschhorn, "Sarah and Hagar."

No one tries to brush it all away
or rushes into glib forgiveness.

. . .

a Hamas sniper, a Mosad assassin fall
to their knees, rocking; each one cries,
"I was only defending my—my—"
Into the arms of each,
Hajar and Sarah place a wailing
orphaned infant. Slow moaning
fills the air: Atone, atone.

The "wailing goes on for ages," until finally the family drama plays itself out and the moment for new stories begins:

Sarah laughs again, more deeply.
Abraham is radiant. Everyone, this time
around, can recognize
in the eyes of every other,
the flickering light of the Divine.[4]

May it be so!

4. Kahf, "All Good."

2

Just Beans

On a Friday afternoon almost forty years ago, I was one of a little band of Jewish and Christian professors and graduate students from Philadelphia who found ourselves in a peaceful village in the south of Germany. We were on a month-long tour of the country, speaking with Germans about post-Holocaust theology. I spent the night in a German Christian's home with another member of our group, my professor, Rabbi Zalman Schachter-Shalomi. Reb Zalman was a refugee from the Holocaust who, as a teenager forty years before, had fled the Nazis for New York. This was his first trip back to Europe.

As the sun began to set, I wondered: how would Reb Zalman observe the Sabbath? I knew he would neither drive nor spend money for the next twenty-four hours, but those were just the prohibitions. What about all the positive practices related to this holy day? On one level, the Sabbath simply happens: it starts every Friday at sundown. On another, the Sabbath is something we must create. We Jews speak about "making *Shabbas*." How would Reb Zalman, visiting the country that had engineered the near destruction of our people, make *Shabbas*?

Being in Germany was not easy for Reb Zalman. Our hosts had been children during the war; their parents had been adults. Our group was taking our first tentative steps toward dialogue between Germans and Jews.

Now, more than most times, we truly needed the Sabbath. And here, more than in most places, we would have to make it ourselves.

Everything about that Friday afternoon convinced me that the start of this Sabbath would be awkward, even lonely and sad. We were strangers in a very strange land. I felt keenly the alienation of being in a place that had so recently been filled with hatred toward *Shabbas* observers. Reb Zalman, however, saw something different. Unlike me, he knew just what to do.

He asked the young daughter of the family to run to the bakery and buy two loaves of braided egg bread. This was a simple request; that type of bread, known by Jews as challah, is common in Germany. Challah is one of the three ritual items, along with candles and wine, that Jews bless at the start of the Sabbath. Off she went, and soon returned with the bread. Smiling, she exclaimed, "I got the last two in the store!"

In the light of the setting sun, Reb Zalman lifted his hands and placed them on the girl's beautiful blonde head. He began to recite in Hebrew the traditional blessing that parents give their daughters on the eve of the Sabbath: "May God bless you like Sarah, Rebecca, Rachel, and Leah." He then translated the words into his native Viennese German. For Reb Zalman—and for me—the Sabbath had arrived.

As Reb Zalman gave the blessing for Jewish daughters to a German child he barely knew, I learned something about ritual and about the life of faith. I learned that the paraphernalia of ritual is less important than the intention.

The next evening, as the stars came out, Reb Zalman picked a fragrant weed from the garden, found some grapes in the refrigerator and lit a match. In doing these acts, he brought together the three symbols required to bid farewell to the Sabbath. While these were not the spice box, kosher wine, and special candle the ritual requires, they did the job. But what really made *Shabbas* that week was Reb Zalman's *hesed*, the very heart of faith.

Hesed, a word that appears 248 times in the Bible, has been translated in many ways: mercy, kindness, goodness, love, and, most often, lovingkindness. Of all the qualities attributed to God, perhaps the most important is *hesed*. We read in the Torah that God requires us to "walk in God's ways" (Deut 10:12), and rabbinic commentaries have featured *hesed* as chief among them. For the rabbis, *hesed* was more than a feeling; it was a doing. God's loyal love for his creatures spills out into our loyal love for God. That love gets expressed in this life in acts of lovingkindness: feeding the hungry, dowering the bride, visiting the sick, burying the dead (Talmud, Sotah, 14b).

Because Reb Zalman understood that God's *hesed* is not restricted to Jews, he extended *hesed* to all people, including the young girl who helped him to bring in the Sabbath. I recall Reb Zalman commenting once that the French make cassoulet, the Mexicans chili, the Jews cholent—but, in the end, they are all just beans. Reb Zalman did not deny differences between cultures; we don't all, deep down, agree on religious truth. In fact, Reb Zalman relished religious differences, drawing an analogy to organs of the body, each with a different function. We would not want the entire body to be a liver; we need a heart, lungs, and skin. Differences should be celebrated because, like the body's organs, they combine to create a more vital world.[1]

Yet even while we enjoy the varied tastes of cassoulet, chili, and cholent, at bottom, each dish is just beans. And, at bottom, aren't we all really not so very different from one another? As children of Adam and Eve, we share a common humanity. We also share a common quest: to meet life's challenges with as much integrity and grace as we can. Religions sometimes obscure our commonalities, insulating us from people who are different, even teaching us to fear them. But our own *hesed*-infused religion can help us overcome our fears and see clearly that those who differ from us on the surface are, at bottom, just human beings.

In the 1950s, Reb Zalman, then a recently ordained Hasidic rabbi, was a man of deep *hesed*, but he had not yet had the opportunity to learn from other faiths. During his graduate studies, he heard about a class taught by the Reverend Howard Thurman, an African American theologian. The class was titled "Spiritual Resources and Disciplines (with Labs)." A strictly observant Jew at the time, Reb Zalman was intrigued, but also frightened, especially about the labs! What might be involved that would be contrary to Jewish law? He went to meet with Reverend Thurman who, noticing Reb Zalman's reluctance, gently challenged him: "Don't you trust the *Ruach ha Kadosh* [Hebrew for "'the Holy Spirit'"]?" Moved by Thurman's Hebrew and by his *hesed*, Reb Zalman realized that he did, indeed, trust.

Reb Zalman's trust would lead him not only to explore Christianity with Reverend Thurman but to study and pray with Sufi mystics, Trappist monks, the Dalai Lama, and many other compassionate and wise people, people with *hesed*. He said that just as going to weddings reaffirmed his own loving marriage, partaking of other religious traditions deepened his love

---

1. To learn more about Reb Zalman's "deep ecumenism," see "Deep Ecumenism."

for God. While Jewish traditions remained his primary path, those profound interfaith conversations and even engagement with some practices enriched his understanding of Judaism and enhanced his own spiritual life.

He once shared that in moments of despair, he would sometimes lie down and sing an old African American spiritual, one that dates back to the era of slavery:

> Sometimes I feel like a motherless child
> Sometimes I feel like a motherless child
> Sometimes I feel like a motherless child
> A long ways from home
> A long ways from home

In such moments, we are all, indeed, just beans.

3

It's Not that Complicated

In 2010, a group of Muslims proposed building a community center in downtown Manhattan. Because the location was not far from the site of the 9/11 attack on New York City, right-wing opponents took the opportunity to launch a campaign against the so-called "mosque at Ground Zero." So successful was their rhetoric that even the Anti-Defamation League of B'nai B'rith, a Jewish organization dedicated to fighting bigotry against all people, sided with the hatemongers. They found compelling an analogy to the Carmelite sisters who wanted to build a chapel at Auschwitz. Sacred ground, in their view, belonged to the victims and their survivors. Anyone connected—even remotely—to the perpetrators should stay away out of respect. "It's complicated," they said.

I did not agree with that view when the topic was Auschwitz, and I found it even more problematic when applied to this situation. Muslim Americans had not attacked New York City on 9/11. The implication that they needed to respect this "sacred ground" was simply a way to "otherize" a religious minority, one that was struggling to find its place in the American religious landscape.

As a Jew, my response was simple. I thought Jews should have unambiguously supported the Islamic center (and supported it even it *had* been a mosque). Our role was to stand with the people of goodwill who wanted to build the Islamic center. I found my own analogies closer to home. Jews in America have experienced what it means to be a religious minority in this society, a society whose ideals should include us all but whose reality sometimes falls short.

In the years immediately following World War I, more than half the Jews in America were foreign-born. They were viewed with suspicion, along with other foreigners, by some who began to advocate to radically restrict immigration. (By 1924, they were successful.) A revived Ku Klux Klan, dormant since 1870, gathered force. Within the context of rising racism and xenophobia, bigotry was directed against Jews who were accused by some of being foreign agitators, or "reds." In 1920, Henry Ford, the leading industrialist in the country, introduced to American readers *The Protocols of the Elders of Zion*—an infamous antisemitic text—printing the first of a series of articles titled "The International Jew: The World's Problem," in newspapers that he owned and widely distributed. Never before (or since) have Jews in America felt so vulnerable.

Not unlike Muslim Americans today, Jews were a diverse community that sometimes disagreed over strategies and tactics. Should they consider litigation? Perhaps, some suggested, Joseph Jacobs's recently published *Jewish Contributions to Civilization* should be widely distributed. Others thought to counter, point by point, the lies in the antisemitic literature. Fortunately, the Jews were not alone; others had their backs.

A socialist author, John Spargo, organized a petition bearing the signatures of President Wilson, William H. Taft, Cardinal O'Connell, and 116 other widely known Christian men and women. Signers included church leaders, secretaries of state and university presidents. Among those who lent their names were William Jennings Bryan, Clarence Darrow, and W. E. B. Du Bois.

Another episode, coming from World War II, shows that Jews continued to struggle for acceptance, even as some Americans stood up in solidarity with us. Rabbi Roland Gittelsohn, the first Jewish chaplain in the US Marines, served with the fighting men on Iwo Jima. At the end of thirty-five hellish days of massive losses, the Protestant chaplain in charge of the division planned an interfaith service to dedicate a cemetery on the island for the fallen troops. He asked Rabbi Gittelsohn to preach.

While some of the Protestant chaplains supported the idea, a majority felt that a Jew ought not be praying over Christians. It was a time of grief and high emotions. In the end, three separate services were held: a Jewish service, a Catholic service, and a Protestant service. But several of the

Protestant chaplains boycotted their own service and attended the small Jewish one to show support for the Jews. They were so taken with Rabbi Gittelsohn's words on that occasion that they asked him for a copy of the sermon. Even without the Internet, the text went "viral" and ended up becoming a famous document of the war, inserted into the Congressional Record and reprinted multiple times. Interfaith services eventually became standard operating procedure in the military.

Rabbi Gittelsohn's sermon still inspires: "Here lie officers and men, Negroes and Whites, rich men and poor, together. Here are Protestants, Catholics, and Jews together. Here no man prefers another because of his faith or despises him because of his color. Here there are no quotas of how many from each group are admitted or allowed."[1]

I like to think that were I a Christian in 1921, I would have signed that petition (or even have helped organize it). If I had been a soldier at Iwo Jima, I hope I would have attended the Jewish service with Rabbi Gittelsohn. Knowing what we do now, we can see that the chaplains opposing the interfaith service were voicing the parochialism of the past.

When I looked at the forces gathering against the Islamic center, I—a Jew—knew I needed to support my Muslim brothers and sisters in a time of grief and high emotions. We Jews had been harmed by those who would prefer some and despise others; such people are not our allies. Our history and hope tell us that their type ultimately will not prevail.

The story of religious minorities in America is a story of one group after another moving from maligned outsider to part of the multi-faith fabric of our country. As recently as 1960, John F. Kennedy's Catholicism presented a problem for some when he ran for president. Yet the issue barely came up by the time John Kerry—also a Catholic—ran not even fifty years later. Where once only Protestants served, today the Supreme Court of the United States has just one Protestant member. The rest are Catholics and Jews! America has surely stumbled along the way—and today shows signs of stumbling again—but I believe that the "arc of history" is inclined toward a more respectful, unified, and accepting society. I want to be on the side of the future.

1. Feldberg, "Rabbi Gittelsohn's Iwo Jima Sermon."

4

Getting to Know Zuleikha

———————

Do you remember the line drawing of an old woman who, if you shift your eyes a fraction of an inch, suddenly appears to be a beautiful girl with a hat? I thought of that perceptual illusion when I was studying the Joseph narrative with a group of emerging Jewish and Muslim religious leaders. We chose the story deliberately. Both traditions cherish the tale of Joseph/Yusuf, a man who was himself an emerging leader, and from a family of siblings that faced the challenge of reconciliation, the very challenge facing the "children of Abraham"—Jews, Christians, and Muslims. Little did my Jewish colleagues and I know that studying the Joseph story with Muslims would introduce us to a new way of looking at this character. Of course, interfaith encounters often yield what is least expected.

Our group knew that the Joseph/Yusuf story looms large in both of our sacred Scriptures: it is the longest single, continuous narrative in Genesis devoted to one character (391 verses). The story absorbs us for four full weeks in the synagogue cycle of Torah reading. In the Quran, an entire chapter, chapter 12, almost a hundred verses long, tells the tale of Joseph—the longest sustained story in the Quran. The text refers to it as "the best of all stories." We knew, as well, that traditions about Joseph have traveled between Jews and Muslims since the very beginning of Islam. Jews and Muslims have borrowed extensively from one another in ways that are impossible to untangle.

But we Jews did not anticipate how important the story of Yusuf and his Egyptian master's wife was to Muslims. In the Torah, the episode of Joseph and Potiphar's wife (Gen 39) seems undeserving of much reflection. Jacob's son, Joseph, sold into Egyptian slavery by his brothers, becomes a servant in the home of Potiphar, one of Pharaoh's officials. The mistress of the house (she is not given her own name in the Torah) attempts to seduce Joseph. When she fails, she falsely accuses him of rape. It is not clear whether she really desires Joseph or is just plotting to get him into trouble. In any case, as far as Genesis is concerned, she seems to be a plot device to get Joseph into jail, so that his story can proceed.

Rabbinic commentary expands on the story but does nothing to improve our impression of the nameless "Mrs. Potiphar." In fact, some of the midrashim made her even more reprehensible, extending her pursuit of Joseph into prison! The commentators seem to have little interest in understanding this woman and what could have motivated her to launch a vendetta against the young man working in her household. In the Jewish mystical tradition, she becomes lust and evil personified, with Joseph the model of restraint. The narrative of two people then becomes a cosmic drama between good and evil.

In the Quran, however, the story has a very different feel. The (still) unnamed seductress, utterly besotted by her passion for the irresistible Yusuf, elicits sympathy. She tries to defend herself, to show those around her that she was a victim of Yusuf's overwhelming beauty. Anyone would be rendered helpless if they had laid eyes on this man! When she gathers the women of the city for a meal, their first sight of Yusuf causes them to accidentally "cut their hands" while preparing food and cry, "God save us! This is no mortal!"

Muslim commentator Ibn Kathir explains: "They thought highly of him and were astonished at what they saw. They started cutting their hands in amazement at his beauty, while thinking that they were cutting the fruit with their knives." Folklore expands upon this tale, making the women so lustful that some of them go into spontaneous menstruation. The knives, round fruit, and emissions of fluid are all not-so-subtle images of sexuality. It is a juicy story the Torah knows nothing about, but it's too good for the Jewish midrash to leave out. So they borrow it! In the Jewish version, the fruit is an etrog—a particular citrus fruit—and in some later Muslim versions, the fruit has a name as well: etrog!

In the Quran's telling, Potiphar's wife then makes a confession, a detail we never hear in the biblical account. Yes, she concedes, I solicited him, but he abstained. How humiliating it must be to confess such a rebuff to the world. We understand her powerlessness in the face of her desire for this young man. Like many of us, she takes out her anger and pain on the person she most loves. Yusuf, determined to maintain his virtue, chooses prison, so as to be safe from her and, perhaps, from himself.

In the final scene in the Quran, Yusuf is released from prison, and the wife reappears. She confesses again: "I do not claim innocence for myself. The self is an advocate of vice, except for those who have attained mercy from my Lord. My Lord is Forgiver, Most Merciful" (12:53). With these words, the nameless wife of Yusuf's master disappears from the story. But not forever!

In the post-Quranic tradition, Potiphar's wife gains a name: first Ra'il and then, more consistently, Zuleikha. Interest in her love for Yusuf (and perhaps his love for her) mounts over the centuries. The unconsummated passion of this couple becomes a model of chaste love. In the mystical tradition of Islam, Zuleikha becomes a symbol of longing, of desire that is never quenched. She is a stand-in for the human soul that pines to be united with God. Poets flocked to the tale. The fifteenth-century Sufi poet Abd'el-Rahman Jami wrote a magnificent book-length poem, *Yusuf and Zuleikha*.

In the nineteenth century, Jews translated Jami's poem into Judeo-Persian and lavishly illustrated the poem with beautiful drawings. So lovely is the artwork that in 2008, the Jewish Theological Seminary chose those pictures to illustrate each page of its annual calendar. Zuleikha appeared month after month in Jewish homes, painted a century and a half ago in what is now Iran, drawing upon a Muslim poem inspired by the Quranic version of the Joseph story.

Hearing new and different versions of a familiar story helped me forge a bond with a character with whom I had never felt the slightest connection. The process moved me from judgment to compassion. Getting to know Zuleikha reminded me why I love interreligious engagement. It is good for us to listen to each other's versions of the stories we share—not only our stories of sacred texts, but also our stories of history and even of current events. We can each tell our stories with great authority as we have been taught to tell them. But looking back at the rich history of "narrative migration," I see how much more interesting and beautiful a story can be if we listen to one another.

Interfaith learning can enrich the way we live our personal lives as well. Zuleikha is with me daily. How many versions of a person's story are hidden from me? What would happen if I moved my head an inch and took another look?

5

What I Have Learned from Christians and Muslims

You may be wondering why a rabbi spends so much time with people from other faiths.

It all started in the spring of 1974. As a college senior, I saw a flyer about a conference at New York's Church of St. John the Divine. I put on my backpack and took the bus down from Connecticut to a gathering called "Auschwitz: Beginning of a New Era?"[1] That conference set my course for many decades. I already knew I wanted to go to rabbinical school, but now I knew, too, that I wanted to be part of the enterprise of these faithful Christians who were grappling with the role of their church in the Nazi Holocaust. A few years later, I moved to Philadelphia to begin my studies at the Reconstructionist Rabbinical College and Temple University, where I could pursue a PhD in Jewish-Christian relations.

The two schools were located just one subway stop away. When my schedule was tight, I could run the six blocks between the two schools. As I traversed those blocks during my five years of study, I often felt like I was moving between two worlds: the world of *wissenschaft*, the academic study of religion, and the world of a more—for lack of a better word—spiritual pursuit.

1. Fleischner, *Auschwitz*.

Here is the irony: the historical critical work—the academic work—was happening at the seminary, an institution that in those days was heavily steeped in that kind of scholarship (this is no longer the case), and the passionate engagement with religious texts was happening (at least for me) at the university in the religion department. The activity of interfaith engagement proved to be the central practice that contributed to my formation as a religious leader.

At Temple University, I worked with a group of Christian teachers who were on a mission—not the old-style mission of conversion, but a Christian mission that was new in the 2,000-year history of the church. They approached these questions not just as scholars but also as engaged Christians. The question of Christianity's complicity in antisemitism was a burning personal concern for them. Like their counterpart, Krister Stendahl, the Swedish bishop and scholar at the Harvard Divinity School, they desperately wanted to "sing their songs to God without telling dirty stories about others." This was more than just a search to understand the relationship between Judaism and Christianity. My teachers realized that something had gone terribly wrong in that family dynamic, and they wanted to help shape the future course of Christianity with attention to its implications for Jews and others.

This turned out to involve a new vision of Christian faith itself. Explorations of history soon turned to rewriting liturgy and reconstructing theology. My Catholic professors, Leonard Swidler and Gerard Sloyan, began working with the townsfolk of Oberammergau, Germany, helping to rewrite their 800-year-old passion play to remove the anti-Judaic elements. Another one of my professors, Paul van Buren, set out to rewrite the theology of his Protestant teacher, Karl Barth. I learned that academics can become part of the work of repairing the world.

And I learned more. Our religions evolve in relationship to others. While the faithful do not usually call attention to this process (in fact, they usually conceal it), we Reconstructionist Jews aim to be transparent about it. I knew that my religious movement expected, indeed encouraged, us to consciously put our own stamp on the evolution of our tradition. I had previously considered such evolution in terms of particular issues: the role of women, the inclusion of gays and lesbians, the creation of new rituals, prayers, art, and traditions. Now, in the post-Holocaust journey to reconstruct Christianity, I learned that a religious tradition can also evolve in response to an awareness of the religious "other." I was not entirely sure how that applied to me and the liberal Judaism of my community. In the eighties and nineties, the work was mostly about helping the Christians get their house in order.

That is, until everything changed.

The change began, like many other transformations in our world, on September 11, 2001. After recovering from our shock and realizing our ignorance, some of us Americans began a piece of work that was new for us: encountering Islam. Within months, the interfaith panels that used to feature a Protestant, a Catholic, and a Jew were now featuring a Christian, a Jew, and a Muslim. Where once I had been confident of the dance steps, I now found myself stumbling through the challenges of a new interreligious encounter, navigating a steep learning curve. I was painfully aware of my ignorance, and hungry to learn more.

I was also aware of my privilege. Jews had a "seat at the table" in the American religious establishment. What would it mean to move over and make room for someone else? When I traveled to Germany in 1980, I met the children of gutsy people whose faith had helped them transcend their times. I also met the children of people who had remained bystanders and were now painfully rebuilding their own faith. In those experiences, I came to understand that our religious traditions are only as vital as their ability to move us to perform acts of solidarity and pursue justice.

My time with Muslim friends and colleagues has given me many gifts. I have learned much about religion and the life of faith. The simple trust in God that I see in some Muslims moves me. My own faith tends to be so much more argumentative. The graciousness of Muslim hospitality has challenged me to up my own game and, at the same time, to appreciate how opening one's home and feeding guests is a spiritual practice.

Some of what I learned has brought me back to traditional Jewish ideas that, as a progressive Jew, I had abandoned. For example, young Muslims introduced me to the power of memorizing sacred language. At conventions of the Islamic Society of North America, I watched children under the age of thirteen recite passages of the Quran from memory with pride and devotion. In my own circles, we had shunned memorization as old-fashioned, uncreative, rote learning. But the joy in those children's faces told me we were losing something important.

In a similar way, I watched Muslims as they knelt five times a day, and I thought: Why don't I have more embodied ritual? We Jews do a lot of our spiritual practice from the neck up: read, study, discuss, repeat. Judaism includes embodied ritual, of course, but I had left it behind with the more traditional Jews. For example, while I say a blessing before eating (when I remember), ritually washing my hands had never been my tradition, or that of my community. Yet it is precisely the physicality of washing that compelled me when I observed it among Muslims.

Even Jews who have strayed far from Jewish tradition often maintain the custom of fasting once a year on Yom Kippur. As a rabbi, I have thought about the meaning of that fast—especially when I'm called upon to speak about it in on the evening of Yom Kippur when the fast begins. I have learned much from Muslims, who fast for the month of Ramadan, about the spiritual meaning of going without food and water for a period of time, wisdom I freely borrow to enhance my own teaching.

Encountering Muslims has taught me the importance of head garb. For most of my life, I could count on my fingers (and maybe a few toes) the times I had donned a *kippah* (skull cap). When I was younger, this was not something women or girls did. It was a male custom, plain and simple. Later, when some Jewish women began to wear the *kippah*, I didn't even consider it—I didn't even own a *kippah*. In fact, I rarely thought about head coverings at all.

Except, of course, when talking with my Muslim sisters. With them, I had many, many conversations about covering the head—their heads. Among my Muslim women friends, some cover and some do not. Some covered in the past and now do not; others never covered before and now are considering it. What I had learned from these discussions is the power and the complexity of that decision, especially for those from a minority religious tradition, especially for women. But in all those conversations, I never once considered how it might relate to me as a Jew.

Until recently. In the current political climate in America, two things have become increasingly clear to me. First, I am going to have to ramp up my spiritual practices in order to sustain my spirit, keep my heart open, and be more mindful—minute to minute—of how I want to show up in the world. I need to find stronger ways to connect heart and hand. Second, I noticed that the Jews with whom I am most aligned politically do not often signal their Jewishness to the world. Some may carry a bit of fear and shame about Jewishness. After some honest reflection, I realized that was true for me, too. It was time to get over it.

As an older, white woman, I walk through the world with a lot of privilege. Where I live, I can wear my identity proudly and without fear. That is not true for many people—including some of my Muslim sisters—and it may not be true for Jews in every place and for all time. But for now, for me, it is a freedom I want to embrace. Putting on my *kippah* has become a ritual act, an occasion to think about my reasons for doing the work I am doing, to consider to whom I am accountable.

Finally, my learning with Muslims has greatly enhanced my understanding of pilgrimage. The importance of the *hajj* for Muslims is difficult to overstate. Since the practice is based on the life of Abraham, our shared ancestor, it particularly moves me. Muhammad Iqbal, a modern Muslim writer often called "the spiritual father of Pakistan," interprets leaving home for the *hajj* as an opportunity to break from habit, routine, and repetition. It reenacts Muhammad's—and before him, Abraham's—choice to break with the parochial birthplace and go off to establish something new. Iqbal compares the myth of eternal return with the idea of the pilgrimage, of moving forward with intention in our lives.[2]

While the stories of Abraham, Sarah, and Hagar contain deeply problematic aspects, a particular dimension of their lives can actually serve us well: each had the faith and courage to go on a journey, to walk into something new. I can embrace them as model travelers into new terrain. It is the idea behind the *hajj* that has taught me to honor something powerful about these ancestors' legacy and to participate in a newly created ritual that brings their children together in a twenty-first–century "*hajj*." For the last fourteen years, I have been part of an Interfaith Walk for Peace[3] in my city, a walk that resonates with me as *hajj*. We walk together—Jews, Christians, Muslims, and more—from a mosque to a synagogue to a church. As we spend the afternoon journeying through a city neighborhood, we affirm our connection to our shared ancestors' journeys, and we affirm our faith that we can move forward in our lives and in our world.

2. Bianchi, *Guest of God*, 23.

3. Philadelphia Interfaith Walk for Peace and Reconciliation, http://www.interfaith-peacewalk.org/.

6

Truths

M y ninth grade social studies teacher changed my life. It was the fall of 1966, and Mrs. Robbins began class by announcing, "I am going to teach you how to think." She then handed out an article from *The Saturday Review* by Theodore Sorensen. "The Looking-Glass War of Words" was a fictitious document made up of arguments in favor of the Vietnam War, some by American sources and some by Communist. They were eerily indistinguishable.

Sorensen's point was not that the American and Communist statements were equally true, but rather that words hurled across a divide often have the quality of reflections in a mirror, similar phrases and ideas but from an opposite point of view. Given that reality, we should at least stop to consider how the world looks through the other's eyes.

Mrs. Robbins wanted us to learn how to think about the rhetoric that most Americans—including many of our parents—believed about the Vietnam War. She taught us that wars are fought with words as well as with guns and bombs. Most important, she impressed upon us that just as you have to keep your wits about you in the midst of a war zone, so, too, you should stay mindful when you are immersed in a war of words.

In July 2014, I traveled to Israel with a group of rabbis during what turned out to be an Israeli invasion of Gaza. As I listened carefully to both Israelis and Palestinians, I tried to keep my focus not on the immediate war in Gaza but rather on the underlying conflict. Who started this round of violence? The answer depended entirely on where you began the story. Arguing about who was most at fault seemed less important than digging into what is at stake for Palestinians and Jews. This topic required a deep look into both the past and the difficult-to-imagine future. I found myself thinking about Mrs. Robbins and her looking-glass war of words.

The Israelis said: "We offered them a deal in Oslo, and they gave us the Second Intifada."

The Palestinians said: "Abbas kept the West Bank quiet since the end of the Second Intifada, and they gave us more settlements."

In this looking-glass war of words, we see an endless cycle of accusations, one often the mirror image of another. And then there are claims that are indistinguishable.

Both said: "No country in the world has endured what we have endured. The world feels too little compassion for our narrative. World media are biased against us. The other side rejoices when we suffer. The other side teaches its children to hate us."

Both said: "Jerusalem is ours! We have no other country."

One of my favorite stories from rabbinic tradition tries to explain why truth is so hard to discern. The midrash begins with a question raised by Genesis 1:26: "Let us make man in our image." The question is simple: Who is God talking to? In the imagination of the rabbis, God is speaking to four ministering angels. The angels, like human beings, were not of one mind; they were as prone to argue as the rabbis telling the story. Some of them said that God should create human beings, and some argued that God should not:

> Lovingkindness said, "Let him be created, because he will dispense acts of lovingkindness."
> Truth said, "Let him not be created, because he will be full of lies."
> Justice said, "Let him be created, because he will perform acts of justice."
> Peace said, "Let him not be created, because he is full of strife."

The vote was tied, two in favor and two opposed. "What did God do? God took Truth and cast it to the ground." With Truth out of the way, the vote was now two to one in favor. Even so, the angels could not let go of a good fight. So God snuck away and created Adam. He then reappeared and asked, "Why are you still arguing? Adam is already made!" (Genesis Rabbah 8:5).

What did I learn from this story? First, the rabbis saw human beings as problematic creatures that almost did not make it into creation. Second, only when Truth was exiled could God go through with the plan. Third, while Lovingkindness, Justice, and Peace are still intact as heavenly ideals, when Truth landed on earth, it shattered into many pieces. We can each get a piece of the truth, but in our arrogance we often assume that our tiny piece of the truth is the whole truth.

This midrash tells us that we need to focus less on Truth, since we each have only a piece of it, and more on Lovingkindness, Justice, and Peace.

That 2014 summer in Tel Aviv, an Israeli colleague and I went to a gathering of Palestinians and Jews who had lost loved ones to terror and war. These people live their lives at the emotional Ground Zero of the conflict, and have chosen, since 1995, to work together for peace and reconciliation. Today there are 600 families in the Israeli Palestinian Bereaved Families for Peace. Each night during the war, they held an outdoor listening circle for anyone who wished to participate.

The group had created a short video and projected it on a screen. Each frame showed one person, a Palestinian or a Jewish Israeli, saying, in a deeply serious tone, "We don't want you here!" They seemed to be speaking at one another, saying the same hostile words across enemy lines. It looked like a looking-glass war of words. But in the last frame, we realized that we had been fooled. They now spoke the same words, but in unison: "We don't want you here! We don't want any new members in our group united by the death of loved ones!" The final frame said, "All the participants, Israelis and Palestinians, lost a family member to the conflict.[1]

1. "We Don't Want You Here."

7

Walking Humbly

He has shown you what is good:
to do justice, to love kindness and to walk humbly with your God.

—MICAH 6:8

The word "and" trails after every sentence. Something always escapes.

—WILLIAM JAMES

Humility? Do we have to go there? It is hard for some of us to see humility as a positive trait. Haven't we been told how important it is to have self-esteem? When I began learning about Mussar, a Jewish practice of character cultivation, I found that many of my fellow students—especially women—had a difficult time with this virtue.

"I beat myself up to too much already," said one woman. "I think religion has made all too many people overly humble and accepting."

But here it is in the text: "walk humbly with your God." In every book about character, humility appears as one of the qualities of soul that we should cultivate. And for good reason. The medieval Jewish writer Bahya

Ibn Pakuda, author of a beloved Mussar text, *Duties of the Heart*, suggests that humility is the very foundation of a virtuous character. This makes sense. If we are going to investigate the state of our soul, we need to be humble enough to acknowledge our deficiencies.

The Alter of Novardok, one of the famous rabbis of the Mussar movement of the nineteenth century, instructed his students to go into a bakery and ask for nails. Why such a strange task? The standard explanation: to crush their egos. Their humiliation would give them a proper sense of themselves as contemptible.

Alan Morinis, a contemporary Mussar writer, has a different understanding. He believes that the point of the bakery exercise was for the students to learn to get along without the good opinion of others. We need to give up seeking honor from the outside. What others think of us is irrelevant, as long as we know who we are. We should neither puff ourselves up nor put ourselves down; we should see ourselves clearly. Morinis offers this definition of humility: Occupy your rightful space, not more than is appropriate but also not less.[1]

My teacher and colleague Rabbi Ira Stone provides his own powerful insights into humility. Rabbi Stone is schooled in Mussar and in the work of Emmanuel Levinas, an important Western philosopher and Jewish religious thinker. Stone teaches that, like all the traits to which we aspire, humility is not really about us. Rather, the trait is relational; the focus is on the other people with whom we come in contact. How we see them is the key.[2]

Humility is about taking your mind off yourself (How am I doing? Am I too proud? Too guilt-ridden?) and putting it on the person in front of you. A strong tradition stands behind this approach. The instruction from *Cheshbon HaNefesh*, a nineteenth-century Mussar text, defines humility this way: "Always seek to learn wisdom from every person." This is not original. An older version comes from the Mishnah, a Jewish law code from the year 200: "Who is wise? He who learns from everyone." (Avot 4:1)

In Buddhist teaching, the student is told to look upon each face he encounters as the face of his mother. Thus one cultivates lovingkindness to all. While this may have made sense in traditional Eastern cultures, Buddhist teachers have found that in America this instruction does not work so well. It turns out that Americans are too ambivalent about their mothers!

1. Morinis, "Through a Mussar Lens."
2. Stone, *Responsible Life*, and my lecture notes from his classes.

The Jewish version of this idea uses the student-teacher relationship as the model of a reverential connection. No matter whom you encounter, imagine them as your teacher.

The goal is to train yourself to seek out something worth learning from every person, every encounter. It is possible to detect something of benefit in even the most challenging interaction. There is always a way in which another individual can teach us something.

One contemporary Mussar teacher suggests the following practice. For one month, each time you encounter someone during the course of the day, determine in advance that you will seek to learn one thing from that person. When the encounter is over, write what you learned on a slip of paper and put it in your pocket. By the end of each day, you will have accumulated some learning, and with luck, some humility.

When I started practicing this discipline, I began to notice how I respond to other people. In some cases—say, the person who checks me in at my health club—I tend to treat them as wallpaper. I saw how often my interactions with others, especially colleagues, involved my seeking their approval, saying something they would think was smart or helpful, getting them to think well of me. I also noticed that I spent a lot of time cataloguing others' faults. I was concerned with my own cleverness and the shortcomings of others. But if I think of the "other" as my teacher, such activities are way off target.

When I devote my efforts to learning from the other person, my teacher, I block my craving for honor and my need to judge. By consciously choosing to learn, I am, by this definition, working the trait of humility. And learning itself gives way to honor. We are told to honor a person who has taught us even one verse, one letter (Avot 6:4). So the point of humility is not to think less of ourselves, but rather to live in a way that honors others.

Rabbi Stone sees humility as the perfect "sweet spot" in which there is room for the self and for the other. If there is room for just one of us, I will rush in, taking up as much space as possible, for fear of being effaced. But then there is no room left for anyone else, even for God. Neither should I shrink myself down to nothing. Soul, says Rabbi Stone, is where self and other reside together, and there is room for both.

Something similar happens in the encounter of faith traditions. How can someone with whom we might deeply disagree on matters of belief be our teacher? Every encounter with a person of another tradition, or even with the tradition itself through a book or film, is a chance to learn something, an opportunity to practice humility. Just as we ask ourselves with another person, "Is there enough room in this encounter for myself and for the other?" so we can ask that question about another religion. When I have faith that space is abundant, that my tradition is strong enough (and that I am strong enough) to absorb new ideas, I can practice humility in my relations with those of other faiths. It is a disposition I can then use throughout my life.

When Rabbi A. J. Heschel, the great twentieth-century religious thinker, gave his inaugural address as visiting professor at Union Theological Seminary, he spoke about four dimensions of religious existence: faith, creeds, law, and community. For him, the most significant basis for the meeting of people of different religious traditions was the first dimension. Faith precedes creeds, law, and community. The latter three often are what divide us, one from the other. Faith is an experience of humility; it is what unites us. Heschel wanted us to get back in touch with the place "where all formulations . . . appear as understatements, where our souls are . . . stripped of pretension and conceit and we sense the tragic insufficiency of human faith." He saw this as an experience that would bring us together. He said, "Our individual moments of faith are mere waves in the endless ocean of mankind's reaching out for God."[3]

Interreligious encounter is but one way of exercising the heart muscle that opens in humility rather than closes in judgment when confronted with an other who, while not our friend (at least not yet), is a fellow seeker whose faith is as human and thus insufficient as our own.

A rabbi, who studied at the Novardok yeshiva in Brooklyn as a teenager, reported that they had a coffin in the basement in which people would take turns lying and meditating on their mortality. That feels like the right place to begin.

3. Quoted in Kaplan, *Spiritual Radical*, 283.

8

Others' Stories

―――――――

Recently, I posted on Facebook a picture of a gathering of Muslim and Jewish women: some bareheaded, some wearing a hijab, some with a *kippah* (skullcap), some with a wig (as is the custom among certain Orthodox Jews). One of my Jewish friends—a skeptic regarding Muslim-Jewish friendship—commented on my posting: "Did you discuss at your gathering how Islamic women can win freedom from abuse and oppression in their native countries?" In fact, we had not. As women, as religious minorities, and as Americans, we had many other things to talk about. We spoke about our lives, our families, our practices, our faith, the Israeli-Palestinian conflict, and our hopes for our communities.

Is there oppression of women in Muslim societies? Of course. But my friend, who felt sure she knew what our topic should be, was the victim of what Nigerian novelist Chimamanda Ngozi Adichie calls the "danger of a single story."[1] We learn something about a group of people, but then we think we know more than we actually do. My friend had reduced all Muslims to a single story of the plight of oppressed women in Muslim-majority nations. (I used to think I *knew* about Israeli settlers in the West Bank, until I met some who confused me—in a good way.) Life, of course, is vastly more complex than a single story.

―――――

1. Adichie, "The Danger of a Single Story."

The Torah provides us with many opportunities to challenge single stories, to look through the lens of complexity at what we think we know. For example, in Genesis as Jacob prepares to die, he offers blessings to his twelve sons. The poetic Hebrew of the blessings makes them both tricky to translate and ripe for interpretation. Jacob calls his beloved son Joseph a *ben porat* (Gen 49:22), traditionally translated as "fruitful man" from the root *p-r-h* (to be fruitful), a label that is consistent with the generally positive blessing Jacob offers his son. But the Jewish Publication Society translation of the Torah (1985) renders *ben porat* as "wild ass." That translation takes *porat* to be a feminine poetic form of *pere*—wild ass. As the notes point out, this is consistent with the attribution of animal names to other sons in the passage.

Another biblical character is also called a *pere*. When Hagar first discovers that she is pregnant with a son, she learns that his name will be Ishmael. The Angel of the Lord goes on to say that Ishmael—the father of the Arab nations and the ancestor through whom Muslims trace their connection to Abraham—will be a *pereh adama*, "a wild ass of a man" (Gen 16:12).

The story of Ishmael in Genesis is an ambiguous one. So, too, is the image of a "wild ass," a sturdy, fearless animal who lives in the wilderness, a symbol of a free-roaming existence. Through the ages, Jewish interpretations of Ishmael have largely depended on the social context of the authors. In early centuries, rabbis portrayed Ishmael in a variety of ways—negative, positive, and neutral. After the rise of Islam, the authors' anxieties and fears were reflected in their consistently negative portrayals of Ishmael. In the anti-Arab and anti-Muslim writing of some contemporary Jews and Christians, we often read of terrorists as descended from this "wild ass."

But if you read Genesis 16 (the wild ass of a man) in light of Genesis 49 (the fruitful man), you might wonder if the Angel of the Lord is saying that Ishmael will be, quite simply, the fruitful father of many—not unlike Joseph. Alternatively, Jacob might be saying that Joseph is—like Ishmael—a wild ass of a man. Fruitful father or wild ass? In understanding *pereh adama* as applied to both Ishmael and Joseph, we are invited to give up the single story we have of each: Joseph as fruitful and good, Ishmael as wild and bad. And when we start to see ourselves in these stories, we can acknowledge the truth: we are all descended from both wild animals and fruitful fathers. We are all children of Isaac *and* Ishmael. Ishmael's is not just the story of the wild and wicked "other." It is also my story.

One of the blessings of multiple stories, of attentively listening to others tell their own stories, is a renewed understanding of oneself. As another Nigerian author, Chinua Achebe, has said, we need "a balance of stories where every people will be able to contribute to a definition of themselves."[2]

Of all the methods of interfaith encounter that I know, perhaps the most powerful is storytelling. In my view, the best learning across traditions comes through the sharing of personal stories. In the age of the Internet, multiple tools can help us transcend the danger of old stories, too narrow for the truths of our time. Yet, ironically, our online lives can also reduce our vision, comfortably ensconcing us in "echo chambers" of our choice. When we expand our imagination by attending to many stories—best heard face to face—we learn that the "other" cannot be captured by a single story. We also make more space for more and different stories of our own.

2. Fetters, "Chinua Achebe's Legacy."

9

The Fast of the Firstborn

The year my nephew was three years old, our usually joyous family Seder veered decidedly off-track. Someone once referred to the Passover Seder as "the longest-running play in history." Indeed, for two thousand years, Jews have been gathering to retell the tale of their liberation from Egypt, with ritual words (the script known as the Haggadah) and acts (some ancient and some newly invented). That particular year, a cousin of ours—not a parent himself—thought it would be fun for the children if we dramatized the ten plagues inflicted on Egypt to persuade Pharaoh to free the Israelites.

In fairness to my cousin, that portion of the Seder is often played these days as comic relief for young folks. We were doing fine with the frog puppets hopping around, to illustrate the plague of frogs that overtook the land (Exod 8:2–6), and turning off the lights, to symbolize the days of darkness over Egypt (Exod 10:21–23). But when we got to the tenth plague, the death of the firstborn, my nephew—a firstborn himself—looked aghast at the very mention of the words and cried out, "That could have been me!" Indeed. He got it. Had he been an Egyptian at that time, his life would have been at risk. The three-year-old understood precisely what the Torah wants him to understand.

Even before the Israelites escape their captivity, God instructs them: "When your children shall say to you: 'What do you mean by this service?'

you shall say: 'It is the sacrifice of the Lord's passover, for He passed over the houses of the children of Israel in Egypt, when He smote the Egyptians, and delivered our houses'" (Exod 12:26–27). God follows up with a raft of laws on precisely how "this service" (which will become the Passover Seder) should be carried out. More laws follow, including one stating that first-borns must be sacrificed to God: "Sanctify to Me all the firstborn, whatever opens the womb among the children of Israel, both of man and of beast, it is Mine" (13:2). In other words, the Torah tells us that our liberation required sacrifice and that we will need to sacrifice in turn.

Beginning with the requirement to "Take . . . a lamb" (Exod 12:3), God instructs the Israelite slaves that on the night of the full moon they are to slaughter lambs and place the blood on the doorposts of their homes. The blood will signal that those homes are to be "passed over" while the firstborn children of Egyptians are killed. The slaves are to roast the lambs and eat them in small family groups, dressed for travel and ready to flee.

Those innocent lambs are not the first animals to get mixed up with religious rituals, nor the last. They are part of the human story of worship of the power or powers beyond ourselves, worship that has often involved the sacrifice of life, human or animal. In the traditions of the Abrahamic family—Judaism, Christianity, and Islam—the lambs stand at the beginning of a long line: the animal sacrifices in the Temple in Jerusalem, Jesus as the "lamb of God" (John 1:29; 1 Cor 5:7), and the sheep slaughtered to this day by Muslims across the world on *eid al-Adah*, the day Abraham was prepared to sacrifice his son Ishmael, although in the end an animal died in his stead.

The fast of the firstborn on the eve of Passover continues the theme of sacrifice. This tradition, not found in the Torah or Talmud but developed later, has Jewish firstborns fasting on the day leading up to the Seder. Over the centuries, some clever Jews developed an alternative to actually fasting all day. If you participate in a study session, you may celebrate with a concluding ritual meal that will override the fast. For many years, I have interrupted my last-minute preparations for the Seder to attend synagogue early in the morning of the eve of Passover to participate in such a study session. As a firstborn myself, I feel a special connection to this theme. Had I been Egyptian, my life too would have been at risk.

This tradition grows more relevant to me each year. As Jews rejoice over their liberation from centuries of exile through the creation of the Jewish state of Israel, they need to be reminded that, like the liberation from

Egypt, this boon was not without cost—a cost paid in great part by others, perhaps inevitably, but no less problematically. Not unlike the firstborn Egyptians whose lives were lost so that we might go free.

I confess that substituting study for a fast always seemed illogical. But lately I have come to see the connection. In the original command to sacrifice, we are told to remember the exodus by giving something up, putting on the alter a lamb or our first fruits, or acknowledging that the *peter rechem* (the one that breaks open the womb) must be bought back from God. In fasting, we give up food. When we study, we give up the belief in the satisfactory nature of our own knowledge. We give up our cherished notion that we know everything we need to know.

After many years of engaging in impassioned discussion and debate about Israel and Palestine with Jews and non-Jews alike, I recognize how hard it can be to listen—to really listen—to the opinions of people with whom I disagree. But when I do open myself to being taught by others, I create my own altar, so to speak, and place upon it the illusion that I already have all the information required to be right.

I am grateful for the rituals and traditions of Passover that remind me that others have paid with their very lives for my freedom. For me, one response is to devote myself to learning more and more: about the "other" who is not really so "other," about the complexities of the ongoing conflict in Israel/Palestine and about the work needed to end the shedding of blood.

10

Purim

As much as I resonate with the themes of Passover, my love for Jewish holidays does not extend across the whole calendar. Purim, the Jewish festival that commemorates the story recounted in the biblical Book of Esther, has long been a challenge for me. The Book of Esther tells of a near genocide of the Jewish people that is averted in the nick of time. Even more improbably, the Jews are given power to take revenge on their enemy, which—according to the story—they do with gusto (Esth 9). The tale reflects Jewish anxieties and hopes, dark fears and dark wishes. The book ends with a command to celebrate these events each year. For centuries of Jewish powerlessness, Jews have marked the alleged date of the reversal with costume parties, humorous plays (called *shpeils*), and lots of raucous fun. It is the only day of the year on which Jews are commanded to drink alcohol "until you cannot tell Mordechai [the hero of the story] from Haman [the villain]."

It is remarkable that the Book of Esther is considered a sacred text. The book deals with Jews living in the Diaspora (to be precise, in Persia, today's Iran), portraying a perilous existence where smarts, guts, connections, and a heavy dose of good luck are needed to survive. Purim means "lots," as in games of chance. The message of the book seems to be that Jewish survival is a "dicey" proposition at best, at least if you live outside the land of Israel. We hear little if anything about God or faith in this story.

Many scholars believe that the tale recounted in the Book of Esther is not historical. Indeed, the narrative reads like a farce, a Purim *shpeil*, if you will. The plot is overdrawn, the characters are caricatures, and everything turns out perfectly—at least for the Jews—in the Hollywood ending. At its heart, the story is about our fragile vulnerability as Jews. In response to this reality, the holiday of Purim prescribes laughter and merriment. It stares into the eyes of despair and counsels a cockeyed recognition of the absurdity of it all, recognizing the need to occasionally, very occasionally, let loose and break at least a few rules. For a persecuted minority, living without power to defend themselves, much less take revenge on their enemies, this response made sense.

But what happens when those who would kill Jews and those whom Jews would kill are once again front-page news? How should we interpret the Book of Esther in a time of Jewish power in the state of Israel? Some Jews read the Book of Esther and come away with a clear vision of right and wrong, Jews and their enemies. When my daughters were growing up, I struggled with how much I wanted to let them enjoy a holiday that I found increasingly problematic.

When bloody passions are all too present in the world, the Book of Esther can be dangerous. In 1994, an American-Israeli Jew, Baruch Goldstein, went directly from the reading of Esther in synagogue on Purim to murdering Muslims praying at the tomb of Abraham. After hearing the news, I almost did not make it to synagogue. But I belong to a community that works hard to create the holidays we need out of the holidays we have inherited. That year, even more than most, we needed to redeem the story of Purim, for our children and for ourselves.

Fortunately, the Book of Esther begins with a minor subplot involving Vashti, Esther's predecessor as queen (Esth 1:10–20). The king orders Vashti to appear before him in her crown (perhaps *only* in her crown), and she refuses. That year Vashti became the heroine and focus of the whole event. This ploy continued the holiday tradition of silliness and fun and allowed us to avoid the entire main plot involving death and revenge.

I had never loved Purim, and after 1994 I tried to avoid it entirely. Until 2017. In January, a new US president took office, beginning a reign that appeared both clownish and alarming. Populations that were already marginalized—undocumented residents, Muslims, people of color, sexual minorities—had much to fear. In fact, this new regime did not seem to bode well for any of us. Life in America seemed more chaotic with an unstable leader at the helm. My own sense of security as an American and as a Jew was shaken.

How should I respond to a situation that appeared unpredictable and threatening, mostly for people more vulnerable than I but also—in an unprecedented way, given my privilege—for myself and for members of my own family? Some of my friends were scared, some angry, some despairing, some in denial. Some woke up every morning, ready to work with equanimity and joy. I cycled through all these responses. I tried—along with so many others—to figure out what effective resistance should look like. Signing petitions? Demonstrating in the streets? Calling legislators? Participating in civil disobedience? Organizing unity prayer services? Writing op-eds?

By the time Purim arrived in early March, the holiday had begun to make sense. On Purim, at least, I knew what to do. I would don a silly costume and act as if good and evil were indistinguishable. For once, I actually joined in the spirit of this holy day that insists that the best response to reality is to wallow in ridiculousness—*for one day.*

In a month Passover would come, with its promise of spring and its very serious grappling with slavery and redemption, with the work of human activists and of God. The new year used to be celebrated at the start of Nisan, the month of Passover. Purim, then, is the last gasp of the old year. Before letting it go, we get a chance to sock it in the eye. Some years deserve nothing less.

11

Did Abraham Pass the Test?

A single Torah tale, one that is especially provocative, can yield entire volumes of interpretation—often contradictory. That is the case with the story of Abraham's near sacrifice of his son Isaac on Mount Moriah. Not only Jews and Christians but Muslims as well have taken this story into their hearts and have struggled mightily with its meaning. The story is problematic, in some ways terrifying, and the literature it has spawned is vast. Perhaps foolishly, I will add my voice to the conversation.

I do so because I think the story (and the devotion lavished on it by its readers over centuries) cannot be ignored. First of all, on its face, the narrative makes no sense: God asks Abraham to sacrifice his "only son, his beloved son" (Gen 22:2), the one through whom God's promises to Abraham will be fulfilled. Abraham promptly sets out to do so. Then, at the moment Abraham stretches out his hand with a knife to slay Isaac, an Angel of the Lord calls the whole thing off. We have every reason to be as confused as Abraham himself was, at least according to Rashi's rendition. Rashi imagines Abraham wondering: What is going on here? "Yesterday you said, 'by Isaac your seed will be called.' Then you retracted and said 'Take now your son.' Now you say, 'Lay not your hand on the lad'" (Rashi on Genesis 22:12).

What *is* going on here? As we try to figure that out, we must add one more piece to the puzzle. The Torah states that all this was a test, one that Abraham passed. Why would God propose such a bizarre test? Isn't murder against everything the Torah teaches? And why would Abraham's willingness to be a murderer (of his own beloved son, no less!) prove that he passed a test?

Some contemporary readers simply refuse to accept the text's claim that Abraham has passed a test. In fact, they read the story as a strong warning how *not* to treat our children. The late Canadian Jewish poet and songwriter Leonard Cohen, for example, sees Isaac as a precursor of all those young men sent off by their fathers to bloody ends in wars. In his song "Story of Isaac" he writes,

> You who build these altars now
> to sacrifice those children.
> You must not do it anymore.

Jews, along with Christians and Muslims, have traditionally looked at Abraham as the revered father of their faith. If we want to find our own way to revere Abraham, we need to make sense of the idea that Abraham had passed a test. We need to get creative.

Two great, relatively recent, religious thinkers—a Christian, Søren Kierkegaard, and a Jew, Joseph Soloveitchik—share an understanding of this story. They agree that it seems entirely irrational that God would promise Abraham a future through his son and then ask him to sacrifice that same son on an altar. But, for them, the irrationality is precisely the point. Although the command makes no sense, Abraham, the "knight of faith" (in Kierkegaard's words), understands that God's sense is not the same as ours, and that we need to trustfully surrender to what seems paradoxical to us. That, according to Kierkegaard, is the true meaning of Abrahamic faith. Soloveitchik goes further, arguing that God called off the physical sacrifice because it was no longer needed. "Experientially," Abraham had fulfilled the command. Before he ever reached Moriah, he had made the sacrifice "in the depths of his heart."[1] A sacrifice of Abraham's heart, not of Isaac's body, was the real test that God had set for Abraham. And Abraham passed.

Rashi reaches a similar conclusion, although in more cryptic language. In Rashi's telling, in explaining to Abraham why he has changed his mind, God says, "I did not say slay him, but [rather] bring him up. You have brought him up, now bring him down." In other words, God never intended that Abraham actually kill his son. He wanted proof of Abraham's complete surrender in faith. Once Abraham showed he was willing to make

---

1. Soloveitchik, *Abraham's Journey,* 10–12.

the ultimate sacrifice, the test was passed. Abraham could take Isaac home. So Rashi, Kierkegaard, and Soloveitchik agree that this is a story about faith as obedience.

Perhaps, like me, you don't find this explanation of the binding of Isaac and its understanding of faith completely satisfying. For a few years, in my twenties, I found this perspective appealing; it was a bracing antidote to the mushy liberalism of my environment. But for many years now, I have not resonated with that interpretation of Abraham's sacrifice. Lacking any better way to make meaning of the story, I deemed it one more example of what is wrong with Judaism (and its cousin faiths as well). I tended to agree with Regina Schwartz[2] and other feminists who argue that the story serves as an indictment of patriarchal monotheism. The entire system, based on one authoritarian, male God, they suggest, leads to horrific violence, including the possible sacrifice of one's own children.

I had almost given up on this story when I learned of another way to read it that made sense to me. Scholar Claire Katz explains how the modern Jewish philosopher Emmanuel Levinas reads this story differently from Kierkegaard, Soloveitchik, and Rashi.[3] According to Levinas, the great moment in the drama is not when Abraham decides to heed God's call and take Isaac up the mountain. Rather, Levinas argues, even more astonishing and worthy of honor is that Abraham is able to hear the voice of the Angel and put down the knife. This, according to Levinas, is the test Abraham had to pass. And he did.

For Levinas, the truly important moment in this saga is when Abraham lifts his knife and looks into the face of his son, what Levinas calls his Other. In that moment, he hears the true call of the Divine, a call that cries out to bear that Other's burden (surely not to kill him). When Abraham sees his son's face, he is able to hear, "put down your knife." According to Levinas, in that moment, Abraham experienced a "trace of God."

For thinkers like Kierkegaard and Soloveitchik, we begin with God, the ultimate Other who commands us. For Levinas, however, we begin with the human Other. God comes later. It is only when Abraham truly sees Isaac that he actually hears the call of God, a call that is always to ethical responsibility.

Reading Levinas himself can be tough going. His philosophical writings are dense. But his several volumes of Talmudic commentary are easier

2. Schwartz, *Curse of Cain.*
3. Katz, "The Voice of God."

to read (not easy—just easier). This brilliant philosopher saw in the Talmud's choice of subject matter a claim on human life, a view akin to his own understanding of religion. Rather than abstract philosophy, the rabbis pondered the lives of ordinary people, seeking to find the right way to live in the messy interactions of families and communities. And according to Levinas, all those complex laws and stories, all those debates about the tiniest matters of how to behave, are ultimately ways of talking about God.

I am struck by the insight Levinas provides for Abraham's story. It is amazing that Abraham could surrender to a voice from God to go up a mountain—setting aside, for the time being, what we think of that choice. But it is even more remarkable that he was able, once he set out on that passionate mission, to turn around and to put down the knife. How often are any of us, once embarked on a righteous mission that we believe in, able to attend to the human face in front of us, pull back and say "On second thought, *no!*"

Levinas challenges us to keep alert for those faces or, in the metaphor of the text, to listen for the "voice of the Angel." That is not easy to do.

When I am swept up in some project bigger than myself (the "will of God" as I understand it), that energy can be all-consuming. But there may be an angel calling for something else. The key is to keep checking the faces of people.

There is one catch. We can only see the faces of "Others" we actually encounter, and our tribal instincts run deep. Our natural human tendency is to hang out with people who look, behave, and believe as we do. What about those who look, behave, or believe differently—the ones we tend to render faceless, to fear, exclude, even shun? In his reading of this story, Levinas reminds us that we should strive to give our "Others" a face. This is easier said in aspirational philosophy than done in the messiness of life. (Despite his gorgeous teaching, Levinas sometimes spoke about the Palestinians in ways that seemed to contradict his own dictum.)

In my experience, when people do finally engage with or encounter their "Other," even those they once feared, *face to face*, something often happens that can be transformative. When I have the privilege of creating those encounters for people, I feel like I am bringing more holiness into the world. My own decision points have not been so dramatic as the one Abraham faced, yet I have had the occasion to experience an "Other's" face in a way that interrupted my own self-absorption. I have, in those rare moments, felt the obligation to bear that person's burden as my own. Thanks to Levinas, I experience that moment as a "trace of God."

12

In God's Image

After September 11, 2001, a Jew who lived near Ground Zero noticed that his windowsill was covered with burnt soot from the destroyed towers. He was reluctant to simply clean up, knowing that something of a human body—the temple that once housed a human soul—might be in the ashes. His rabbi agreed and instructed him to carefully wipe the sill with a paper towel, take the towel to the nearest cemetery, say proper prayers, and bury it. Even the last remains of a human being are that sacred!

The reason is simple. As Rabbi A. J. Heschel put it, "Wherever you see a trace of man, there is the presence of God." Heschel invoked this idea—that human beings are made in the image of God—many times during his career. In 1963, in Chicago, American religious leaders held a historic conference to begin to discuss the major moral challenge of their day: racism. Rabbi Heschel delivered the keynote address. An immigrant to America from Hitler's Europe, he was no stranger to racial oppression. Heschel began by invoking Moses and Pharaoh and their "summit" on "religion and race," saying, "The exodus began but is far from having been completed," thus invoking the shared biblical narrative that already was a powerful connection between this Jew from Poland and the final speaker, his future friend and ally, the Reverend Martin Luther King Jr.[1]

---

1. Heschel, "Religion and Race."

Heschel went on to say, "The making and worshipping of images is considered an abomination, vehemently condemned in the Bible. . . . And yet there is something in the world that the Bible does regard as a symbol of God. It is not a temple or a tree, it is not a statue or a star. The symbol of God is man, every man. . . . Man, every man, must be treated with the honor due to a likeness representing the King of kings."[2]

What was Heschel doing with this excursion into biblical thought? Was this a rhetorical flourish, a way to add emphasis to the secular philosophical idea of universal human dignity, the kind of thing you would expect a rabbi to say? Was he invoking the metaphor "image of God" (Hebrew, *tselem elohim*) because he thought the idea of the equality of all human beings could not stand on its own? Was this simply another way for a Jew to build a bridge to an American audience steeped in Christianity? For Heschel, this was not just a way of speaking. It was the very core of who Heschel was and how he fundamentally understood human beings. It was because of the belief in *tselem elohim* that Heschel was in that room giving that speech in the first place.

The term *tselem elohim* appears in the Bible only in the first eleven chapters of Genesis. God creates human beings—and only human beings—in God's image. After human beings disappoint God so completely that they are almost wiped off the earth, after the flood, God repeats the phrase *tselem elohim*. God still wants humans to run the world. Humans can kill animals, but nobody, neither animals nor humans, can kill a human with impunity. One famous and paradoxical verse, Genesis 9:6, establishes the inviolability and sacredness of human life, giving both the warrant for capital punishment and the concept used by the rabbis to effectively abolish it.

It was the rabbis (as well as Christian writers) who developed "God's image" into a key theological concept in a language that spoke to the world in which they lived. The Greco-Roman world had rules concerning the care of the statues of the emperors. Rabbi Hillel refers to this in his famous statement that in going to the bathhouse he is fulfilling a command of God. "If we wash the statues of the king, how much more should I wash my own body!" (Leviticus Rabbah 34:3).

When I was a child, I had a voracious thirst to learn what other people did with their deepest fears and hopes: with their solitude, their sense of connection, and their awe. My family was not big on spiritual practice. Study, however, was a sacred endeavor in our household. So, as soon as

2. Heschel, "Religion and Race."

I could choose my own books, I began reading about the religions of the world. When I was fifteen, I learned something that changed my life, and it happened, of all places, in synagogue school. We were exploring a passage from the Mishnah: "An earthly king stamps his image on a coin and they all look the same. But the King of Kings, God, puts His image on every human being, and every one is different" (Mishnah Sanhedrin 4:5).

That felt exactly right: I was a unique coin, but stamped from the very same "image" as every other. That text made sense to me. No person is more holy than any other. This messy reality with all its wild diversity was actually also a unity, a sacred oneness. Moreover, that idea resonated for me, in the late 1960s, with the great struggle for civil rights, and Heschel's involvement helped me to make the link. Both were saying the same thing: No one is more in the image than anyone else. All the hierarchies we construct are only our imaginings. As the Mishnah put it, "we were all created from one couple so no one can say, 'My ancestors are better than your ancestors.'" At the conference, Heschel found his bearings on the issue of race in America and concluded, "The image of God is either in every man or in no man."[3]

There once was a famous debate between two rabbis over the question: What is the greatest principle in the Torah? Rabbi Akiba appears to clinch it with his answer: Love your neighbor as yourself. Jews and Christians share this theme. Jesus, in both Mark's and Matthew's gospels, refers to this command (along with loving God with all your heart, soul, and mind) as the essence of the Law and the Prophets, and the Reconstructionist prayerbook that I use provides an opening meditation for morning prayers: "Here I am, ready to take on the commandment to love your neighbor as yourself" (Lev 18:19). But Ben Azzai suggests a different answer: the greatest principle in the Torah is that humans were created in the image of God. Ben Azzai quotes the verse: "This is the book of the generations of Adam. From the day God created human being, in the likeness of God did God make them" (Gen 5:1). Ben Azzai says, "This [creation in the image of God] is a principle greater than love your neighbor" (Bereshit Rabbah 24:6).

Jewish theologian Arthur Green often returns to this argument, agreeing with Ben Azzai that creation in God's image is "our most basic message." Green points out, "Some people are easier to love, some are harder. Some days you can love them, some days you can't."[4] But you still have to treat all of them, all the time, as an image-bearer of God. Perhaps Ben Azzai

3. Heschel, "Religion and Race."
4. Green, *Radical Judaism*, 123.

feared that Akiba's chosen principle, love your neighbor as yourself, might be narrowed to only loving one's own community. "Your neighbor" might refer only to Jews, or to people who are kind to you.

What about the stranger?

Recognizing that "love your neighbor" may not be sufficient, the Torah reminds us frequently (by some counts, thirty-six times) to love the stranger, to not oppress the stranger, to be kind to the stranger. The reason: because we were strangers in the land of Egypt. We know the heart of the stranger. But this does not always do the trick. We are wired to see danger and to protect ourselves, and strangers can be dangerous. In particular, those who have been harshly treated themselves may turn around and oppress others. Ben Azzai's expansive principle leaves no room for exceptions. And it doesn't excuse us when our feelings get in the way. However we happen to feel, we must honor a fellow creature.

Ben Azzai can be a good guide. We don't have to *love* everyone, but we do need to see them as images of God; and as images of God, they deserve *kavod*. The word *kavod* comes from the root meaning "heavy," as in taking ourselves and others with great seriousness. This is also the word used in the fourth commandment: honor (*kavod*) your father and mother. In the Bible, God is described as having *kavod*, and God's *kavod* (often translated as "glory") fills the whole world.

As the former chief rabbi of the United Kingdom, Jonathan Sacks, says, we have to recognize the image of God in those who are not in our image.[5] And that is hard to do. The truth is, sometimes it is hard for me to see the image of God in people close to me, in my relatives, friends, and co-workers. How much more so in strangers! This is not such an easy belief to maintain. But I know it is worth trying.

5. Sacks, *Dignity of Difference*, 60.

13

Manna from Heaven

Each Friday afternoon, I spread a tablecloth on my dining room table, place two braided loaves of bread on the cloth, and then cover the bread with another cloth, one of several beautiful, specially designed challah covers we have accumulated over the years. In my first days of rabbinical school, I learned that the custom of blessing two loaves on Shabbat evokes the double portion of manna—the *lechem min ha shaymayim*, or "bread from heaven"—that the Israelites collected on the eve of the Sabbath as they made their way from Egypt to the Promised Land (Exod 16:4–5).

In the version recounted in the book of Exodus, the manna appears under a layer of dew (16:13). But when the same story is told in the Book of Numbers, the manna appears on top of the dew (11:9). Rashi claims that it's easy to resolve this discrepancy: the manna fell *between* two layers of dew! Our Shabbat loaves, nestled between two pieces of cloth, can serve as a weekly reminder that our bounty—the bread we eat and, in truth, all our bounty—comes to us like "manna from heaven."

So the practice of covering our challah can become an occasion for learning.

The Torah tells us that every morning, for forty years, a portion of manna appeared in the wilderness for each person according to his or her habits of eating (*ish l'fi ochlo*)—no more, no less (Exod 16:18). The instructions were clear: each person should gather his or her share each

189

day. Everyone *had* to start each day with just enough for that day. But, as one might expect of former slaves, they ignored the instructions, hoarding more manna than their daily portion. In a dramatic response, this extra manna became infested with worms (16:20).

The question arises: Why did God not just provide all the manna that was needed for a week or even a year? According to the Torah, manna was provided daily so that "you shall see the glory of the Lord" (Exod 15:7). The manna teaches the Israelites to anticipate and then enjoy God's presence each and every day. Our Shabbat "manna," the challah, serves as a similar reminder: we are to sense God's kindness in feeding us *each and every day*. The Talmud teaches: "The Holy One nourishes and provides sustenance for everything from the horns of wild oxen to the eggs of lice" (Babylonian Talmud, Shabbat 107b). So we are taught to ground ourselves in gratitude.

But there is more. Manna plays a role in a dispute between two twentieth-century American philosophers, John Rawls and Robert Nozick. Rawls famously argued in favor of distributive justice, suggesting that we should think of society's goods as a pie to be distributed as fairly as possible. Nozick, however, maintained that society has no right to take and then distribute what individuals produce with their own talents and efforts. Producers of goods have a certain entitlement to what they produce. After all, Nozick wrote, it's not as if the goods appeared like "manna from heaven."

Perhaps not. Yet our talents are not earned; they are God-given, and they would be worth little without the nurturance of parents, teachers, and society. Even within a capitalist system of incentives, much of what we have is "manna." In the United States, we are living with an extraordinary level of wealth inequality. Since 2007, the wealth gap in the United States—already growing since the 1970s—has expanded ever more dramatically and has now reached its highest level since before the Great Depression. In 2016, the average family in the top 1 percent of earners made forty times more than the average family in the bottom 90 percent of households.[1]

Even more troubling, despite many Americans' belief that we live in a land of opportunity, social mobility is in decline. Harvard professor Robert Putnam and his colleagues explore some of the reasons for this stagnation. Children in our country, long before they have a chance to produce (or not produce) goods to which they would be entitled, receive vastly different, and unequal, supports from their environment. In 2015, 13.1 million US children lived in households that lacked consistent access to enough food.

1. Rios and Gilson, "11 Charts."

In the first few years of life, the lack of good nutrition can affect mental, physical, and emotional development. The prospects for getting into a good school, marrying, and having a successful career are ever further out of reach for children from low-income families.[2]

What can it mean, then, when I lift the challah cover each Friday night? Surely, it can become an occasion to experience renewed gratitude for the plentitude with which I am blessed. But it can also serve to remind me that I live in a society that is, shamefully, departing ever more from the manna ideal.

Like the Jews, Muslims have preserved the memory of the manna. In a well-established tradition, the Prophet Muhammad said that "Kam'ah [truffles] is a type of manna, and its liquid is a remedy for the eyes."[3] Would that my Shabbat challah could serve as a remedy of my own "eye disease"— my own un-seeing of what is hard to look at and what I, in my privilege, can so easily keep out of my view. May my "bread from heaven" remind me not to be blind to the gap between my plenty and others' wants, between our current reality and the vision of a more just world.

---

2. Putnam, *Our Kids*.

3. Quoted at http://www.qtafsir.com/index.php?option=content&task=view&id=379.

14

Bearing the Burden of the Other

Father Edward Flannery, a Roman Catholic priest, was walking down Park Avenue in New York City with a Jewish friend at Christmastime. As they passed a huge, illuminated cross, his Jewish friend remarked, "That cross makes me shudder." For Father Flannery, the cross symbolized only universal love. Clearly, he thought to himself, my friend knows something I do not know.

Seeing the cross through the eyes of his Jewish companion led Father Flannery to research and write a history of antisemitism, the first one written by a priest.[1] He completed the book in 1964. The next year, Vatican II (the Second Vatican Council) issued *Nostra aetate* (English, "In Our Time")—the "Declaration on the Relation of the Church to Non-Christian Religions"—in which the Church repented of its anti-Jewish past. Flannery went on to devote his career to Jewish-Catholic relations. He not only came to understand his Jewish friend's burden; he wanted to carry it along with her.

One of my own "Father Flannery moments" took place in 2006, when I was in residence for a week at the Washington National Cathedral with two other women—an Episcopal priest and a Muslim scholar of Islam. We lived together in a cottage on the grounds of the Cathedral. There we ate all

1. Flannery, *Anguish of the Jews*, xi.

our meals, slept, and spent each day reading and talking with each other. At the end of the week, we would give a report of our experiences in a program held in the nave of the Cathedral.

We left the cottage only to attend our houses of worship. On Saturday—with my two sisters in tow—I headed for a Reconstructionist synagogue nearby. I felt sure my colleagues would love my community as much as I did. As we pulled up, my heart swelled with pride. There was a huge banner reading, "Save Darfur!" I thought: *How great that they show concern for people other than Jews!* My Muslim colleague, however, saw something completely different. That banner reminded her of Muslims engaged in killing. The outsized role the Jewish community was playing in protesting those (Muslim) killings aroused her suspicion. As I felt proud, my colleague shuddered.

I felt her burden, and I wanted to bear it with her.

Like many Americans, my first serious encounters with Islam began after 9/11. Before this my interfaith work consisted of the post-Holocaust Jewish–Christian dialogue, and I spent a great deal of energy promoting my community's agendas: "Understand us!" "Do not teach your children to hate our religion!" "Support our causes!" After 9/11, things were dramatically different. Now I needed to understand and protect others and their religion.

My teacher Paul van Buren, a Christian theologian, was fond of saying that the Anti-Defamation League, the watchdog organization the Jewish community developed to combat antisemitism, ought to be funded, staffed, and run by Christians; Jews shouldn't have to do that for themselves or, at the very least, not *by* themselves. He thought that Christians, with their twin commitments to love and justice, should assume some responsibility for combating antisemitism.

As I thought about Muslim-Jewish relations, van Buren's words came back to me. Non-Muslims should be standing up to combat anti-Muslim bigotry. As a Jew, I wanted to work alongside Muslims and bear their burdens with them. So I built relationships with emerging Muslim leaders and asked them to teach me about the challenges facing them. I tried to stand up to the fearmongers and to encourage my fellow Jews to root out the ignorance and bigotry in our own communities.

In this work, I had to face both my ignorance and my privilege. Most of all, I had to grapple with some of my most cherished ideas about my own faith. Father Flannery, Paul van Buren, and other Christian mentors had taught me that this journey of listening to the "Other" would not be a simple matter. Ultimately, it would lead me—as it had them—to see my own tradition in new ways, and to want to transform it.

For example, most Jews have understood the state of Israel as a redemptive response to the horrors of the Nazi Holocaust. Understood in this way, the state of Israel offers the possibility of hope, making the history of the last century something meaningful for Jews, and not just a series of tragic events. The prayer for the state of Israel found in Jewish prayerbooks around the world asks God to bless Israel, "the beginning of our redemption." The Jewish people indeed stepped back from the brink of despair into hope through the creation of a Jewish state.

Each spring, Jews celebrate Israel Independence Day with joyous parades. Close in time, Palestinians observe *Yawm al-Nakba*, the Day of the Catastrophe. Our liberation and hope were their displacement and disaster. I can no longer recite that prayer for the state of Israel nor celebrate that holiday without hearing the voice of the Other, without feeling their trembling. One thing I know for sure: in the years to come, some of us will change that prayer and that holiday. Some of that change is already happening.

American rabbinical students are required to spend time studying in Israel. I teach a class at the Reconstructionist Rabbinical College where students are required to write their theological autobiography. Twenty years ago, many of their theological autobiographies spoke reverently about the special thrill they felt walking the streets of Jerusalem, praying at the Western Wall, ordering a meal in Hebrew, witnessing the ingathering of Jews from all over the world. As the years have passed, though, one or two students, then a handful, now more than half of the students write about the conflict they feel as they've come to understand the perspective of the "Others" who have paid a price for this dream. My students are increasingly involved in peace activism, working for a just resolution of the conflict that speaks to the redemptive hopes of Palestinians.

Activism comes in many forms. In 2010, Sheryl Olitsky, an American marketing professional and the wife of a rabbi, placed a call to Atiya Aftab, a Muslim lawyer. Sheryl left a message saying that she wanted to start a small group of Jewish and Muslim women who would form relationships, one Muslim and one Jew at a time. She hoped they might begin to build trust between their communities. Today, there are 150 chapters of the Sisterhood of Salaam Shalom in the United States.[2] As a founding board member of this organization, I have watched with amazement as, in city after city, Jewish and Muslim women are breaking bread together and telling each other their stories of family and of faith.

Even if we are not yet ready to be one another's Anti-Defamation League or Council on American Islamic Relations, at least we can begin, as Father Flannery has taught us, to listen to others and learn what their burdens might be. Then, even if the steps are small, we can begin to bear them together.

2. See https://sosspeace.org/.

15

No Skipping Steps

E very Tuesday evening for almost a year, I had been sitting with Rabbi Ira Stone and a small group of students, studying a classic text from the Jewish ethical/spiritual tradition of Mussar. Our goal: to cultivate our own virtues so that we could show up in our lives as the best version of ourselves. One day, I arrived in class to see that the synagogue library was crowded with cartons of kosher wine, stacked floor to ceiling, waiting to be picked up by congregants for their Seders. I launched into a sermon on the ridiculous exclusivity embedded in the idea of kosher wine. (For wine to be considered kosher, a non-Jew must not have touched it.) I spoke about xenophobia and universal ethics, and I ended with a lesson on "the image of God in all human beings."

The next week, my fellow student Miki told me how my rant about kosher wine had made her feel. She cared about keeping kosher. She appreciated that I had this noble philosophy that included all humanity, but had I bothered to look at the person right next to me? Did I notice the pain my words were causing her? It was hard to hear what she had to say—difficult, even now, to tell the story.

I think of that experience whenever I hear the Torah tale of Nadav and Avihu, the two older sons of the high priest Aaron who went rogue (it's mentioned twice: Lev 10:1–2; Num 3:4). According to the Bible, these fellows made up their own creative liturgy (as many contemporary Jews do today). Nadav and Avihu brought to God "a strange fire." Then, with no warning, they lay dead at their father's feet.

Clearly, this is a story that needs elaboration. Some interpreters see the death of the priest's sons as positive: Nadav and Avihu established a mystical connection with God, and their souls merged with God's. But most of the tradition sees their young deaths as a punishment. If they had successfully negotiated their encounter with God, they would not have been killed. This leads to the question: What did these brothers do wrong? Clearly, they had a passion to serve God. But something was amiss.

In order to explain the fate of these two young men, commentators search the scanty textual evidence for clues. In their exhaustive search for the crime to fit the punishment, some commentators have noted this: each brother took his fire pan separately. This could imply that they were not really collaborating; they were not working as a team. The Talmudic scholar Shimon Bar Kappara, in his list of four sins for which the brothers died, includes this reason: "'For not having taken counsel from each other,' as the text says, 'Each of them took his fire pan.'" (Leviticus Rabbah 20:10).

Maybe Nadav and Avihu skipped the first step on their way to loving God. To realize our love for God, we first must realize our love for human beings: our family and those closest to us, and then our tribe, and then the stranger. We go to lengths for our own family we would not consider for a stranger, and our love for our tribe is stronger than our love for the more abstract and distant other. All of these are steps in a progression. Maybe Nadav and Avihu skipped the first step along the way.

Lately, I have been wondering if I, too, have been skipping a step.

Like many Jews of my era, I grew up with a strong sense of pride and connection to the Jewish people. In the 1950s and 1960s, the twin pillars of the Nazi Holocaust and the young state of Israel provided a compelling foundation for my sense of communal obligation to Jewish peoplehood. Although my early interfaith work involved participating with Christian scholars in rethinking the anti-Judaism and antisemitism of their heritage, over the years, I began to feel that the problem of antisemitism was not the most pressing issue for me to address. As my teachers who were white Christian Americans (and mostly men) had recognized their own privilege and power, I became more interested in exploring my own privilege as an Ashkenazic American Jew. I believed the Jewish community was holding its memories of suffering too close and for too long. I wanted to encourage Jews to work toward justice for *others*, in particular Palestinians and

Muslims in America. I often argued that we American Jews did not sufficiently recognize our own power, and placed too much emphasis on our vulnerability.

Now, after the election of Donald Trump, I am not so certain. The present moment is, without question, the most challenging many of us Americans have known. We are trying to find our footing in this new reality. For me, this year has provided a new education in "not skipping steps." I am—as they say—evolving as fast as I can. Here is what my evolution looks like.

In the past. I have been in the habit of emailing close Muslim friends and colleagues on the occasion of some especially egregious assault on their community. Now, when the president and the people around him seem indifferent to preserving the memory of the genocide of Jews in Europe, uninterested in threats to Jewish institutions, and willing to entertain anti-Jewish bigotry, the context of isolated incidents of antisemitism has changed. Lately I have received emails from Muslim friends expressing solidarity and concern for me as a Jew.

Those gestures have felt unfamiliar, and even a little confusing, but mostly I have welcomed them. Even more unfamiliar to me—and in some way challenging—has been the call to advocate for my own community. I am accustomed to critiquing my community for its self-involvement and for not showing up in the public square for others, but I have come to realize justice means justice for all (yes, including my own people). After having to explain to some Jews why Black Lives Matter is crucial (not just "All Lives Matter"), I need to remind myself that there is a time and place for "Jewish Lives Matter" and—*in that moment*—to leave it at that.

When vandals desecrated a Jewish cemetery in my city, rabbis—including progressive ones—raced to the scene, held services for their communities, and participated in planning a rally with the Jewish Federation to "Stand Against Hate." I worked to overcome my own complicated emotions provoked by a Jewish gathering that would likely be more ethnocentric than I am comfortable with. In the end, I showed up at the rally proudly and then went on to a second rally that day for the New Sanctuary Movement— a group that works to end injustices against immigrants.

I want to be alert to the dangers of this time for my community, even as I believe there are other communities at far more risk. I am wary of Jews failing to sufficiently acknowledge their actual position in this society. I realize that many of them believe (at least emotionally) that their security could all "turn on a dime." I need to cultivate empathy for them, but also to stay cognizant of the immediate reality: Jews are not the first victims in line at this time.

I hope that our era becomes one in which Jews learn to advocate wisely for themselves even as they acknowledge their connection with other vulnerable groups in our society—Muslims among them. I fear that forces of hate with little sympathy for either of our communities may yet succeed in turning us against one another in ways we have not imagined. I am haunted by the images of Sarah and Hagar, two vulnerable women, ancestral mothers of Jews and Muslims, locked in enmity by forces larger than both of them.

What does all this have to do with kosher wine? Kosher wine acknowledges the difference between Jews and others; it's a distinction that feels unnecessarily parochial to me in the matter of wine. But difference there is. I have work to do to cultivate more compassion for my own tribe, our troubled history, and our particularistic responses.

And then there is my fellow student Miki—the person sitting next to me, the first step on my way to compassion. I need to notice that person, check in with them, and read their face, as I failed to do with Miki. A universalist vision must rest on it all—self, tribe, strangers. Without those pieces, universalism dissolves into a meaningless abstraction, and serving God well becomes even more unlikely.

There is much that is unclear in our country and world today, but here is what I do know. The brothers Nadav and Avihu should have served each other first, then their extended family, then the Israelites, then the world, and then God. No skipping steps.

16

Hope

———————

My friend Imam Yahyah Hendi was born on the West Bank in 1966 and emigrated to America in the 1980s. Back in the 2000s, I invited him to address my rabbinical association at our annual convention, meeting that year in Baltimore. The week of his lecture, a Palestinian gunman shot several religious Jewish students in Jerusalem. During his talk, Imam Hendi spoke of "the gunman who killed our students." Sixty startled rabbis immediately sat up straight in their chairs. *Our* students? What did the Imam mean by *our* students? Had he misspoken?

And then, on face after face, the recognition dawned! The Imam was speaking as if we were already living in the future that we wanted to build together, a future in which both Palestinians and Israelis would count as "ours," in which "our dead" would mean all those who died on *both* sides. The rabbis were riveted by the Imam for the next hour and a half.

All of us need opportunities, every once in a while, to pretend that we are "there," that the future we hope for has already come to pass. We Jews call that a foretaste of the Messianic era. In that time to come, we will all call each other's children "our children."

At no time in my life have I prayed to a God who I believe listens to my prayers, decides whether they are worthy, and manipulates reality to make them come true (well, maybe two or three times, but I was under a lot of stress). Most of the time, I find it hard to understand how people believe in such a God, although I do not disparage their belief. It simply is not mine.

We dwell in mystery. We wake to find ourselves placed on this planet without any say in the matter and stay until we are forced to leave, usually against our will again, never fully understanding it all. In the face of the sheer unknowing that most of readily acknowledge, our religions ask us to make meaning of our time here.

In chapter 6 ("Truths") we discussed the midrash that pictured the angels in heaven arguing about whether human beings should be created. The Talmud tells us that the dispute did not end there. Two sets of rabbis were still debating the question in their own time. For two and a half years, the House of Hillel and the House of Shammai argued: Is it a good thing that God created humans? After the votes were all in, the verdict was clear: it would probably have been better if humans had never been created at all. But, the rabbis concluded, since we *are* here, we had best examine our deeds (Eruvin 13b).

I love that story. Hard as it to believe, it really matters what we do with our lives; we can make them better each year. It's even more difficult to believe that the world is headed toward a final healing. The mystery is not neutral; it is weighted toward redemption. Where do we find dazzling confirmation of this truth? Nowhere. We cheat despair by saying, "God," even when we can't see how the dots of our lives ultimately connect to form a picture. That is why it is called faith. We are asked in the face of the mystery to hope.

Sometimes, I wonder if we are being duped. But then I consider the example of those who have acted on such assumptions—aid workers who enter war zones while others are fleeing, ordinary congregants who spend vacations and summers transforming faith into bricks in building projects for the homeless in our cities. Their lives do not appear to me to be foolish or misspent. Hope doesn't feel like a mistake. In fact, it feels like an obligation.

I have two very young grandsons. There is a great deal we do not know yet about these children or the world they will grow up in. I have been thinking a lot about my hopes for them and for any future grandchildren whom our daughters and their partners will raise.

I hope they will find the world a fascinating place and that important matters will compel their attention and give meaning to their lives. (With luck, these matters will also be something from which they can earn a living.) I hope that they live out the traditional Jewish blessing I have given to each of them, that they will grow to "*huppah, torah and ma'asim tovim*"—that they flourish in relationships, in lifelong learning, and in good deeds. Or, as the great Jewish thinker Sigmund Freud said when asked about the goal of therapy, I hope that they are able to "love and work." Most important, I hope they will spend their lives committing acts of lovingkindness, both random and routine, that they will be among those people who leave the world better than before—or at least knock themselves out trying.

Notice, please, that I did not say that I hope they will be Jewish. Unlike most Jewish grandmothers in the past, I cannot make that assumption. My grandchildren will carry in their genes and in their parental heritage more than one religious and ethnic tradition. In other words, they will be like many twenty-first–century Americans—mutts. A nicer way of saying that is that they will benefit from hybrid vigor. Does it surprise you to know that a rabbi is okay with that?

In fact, I trust that my grandchildren will figure out who they are, and I suspect they may do that more than once in their lifetimes. I realize that identity for their generation will be neither as unified nor as stable as it was as recently as when their parents were growing up. What I do hope is that whether their affiliations are single or multiple, constant or in flux, they will honor what is good in the tradition I have taught to my students and children, some of which I have tried to share in this book.

I hope, too, that they will build a relationship with God and that they will be supported and sustained in that relationship by a community. In my experience, it is really hard to live a life, let alone find God, without a community. I once heard a talk by a scholar of religion, a man who considered himself equally connected to every religion in the world. He sounded terribly lonely. I do hope that my grandchildren will discover a religious tradition that is worth loving and wrestling with over the long haul. (In my relationship with Judaism, I have found the wrestling as meaningful as the loving.)

Mostly, I hope that wherever my grandchildren hang their hats, and for however long, the people they choose to be with are open to ideas outside their own four walls, that they value (rather than fear) difference, and that they hold a generous and compassionate vision for all the others with whom they share their city, country, and planet.

That's all quite ambitious, I know, but my faith as a Jew has taught me the fundamental value of hopefulness. To put it another way, losing hope is a major Jewish heresy. In my effort not to fall into that particular heresy, I find that my immersion in Jewish learning, in the Jewish calendar, and in Jewish prayer and practice helps. In these chapters, I have tried to give you a glimpse of how they have sustained me and how they have strengthened my commitment to justice for all people.

For me, observing the Sabbath, the "foretaste of the Messianic Age" (Genesis Rabbah 17:5 and elsewhere) is one way of keeping alive hope in another world, even if we will never live in it fully. On the Sabbath, we offer no requests, only thanks, because we dwell in the fantasy that we already have everything we need. We are told to do no work because there is nothing to fix.

Joining with people of other faiths is another way I get a glimpse of that world toward which we aspire. We live in a time of much distrust and fear between people of different tribes. But there also exist deep reservoirs of untapped goodwill. We nurture those good impulses when together we do service projects, advocate for common goals, study our sacred texts, make music, share food, pray. When we march together, learn together, tell our stories to each other, we live into the world we hope for.

Most important, we strengthen our "hope muscles" when we dream together—with faith in the eventual triumph of good. Our interreligious experiences should serve to strengthen the belief we share—*because* we are religious people—belief in what appears to be impossible. We can see a way past the challenges of our world. I think of interreligious encounters as a spiritual practice that can cultivate resilience in hard times.

As we say in our Jewish prayer for God's ultimate sovereignty, "May it come speedily and in our day."

Bibliography

Abu Da'ud, Sulayman ibn al-Ash'ath al-Sijistani. *Sunan Abu Dawud*. Translated by Ahmad Hasan. Lahore: Sh. Muhammad Ashraf, 1984.

Adichie, Chimamanda Ngozi. "The Danger of a Single Story." TED Global, 2009. https://www.ted.com/talks/chimamanda_adichie_the_danger_of_a_single_story.

al-Albani, Muhammad Nasir al-Din. *Sahih al-Jami' al-Saghir wa-Ziyadatihi*. Al-Riyad: Maktabat al-Ma'arif, 1986.

al-Bukhari, Muhammad ibn Isma'il. *The Translation of the Meanings of Sahih al-Bukhari: Arabic-English Vols. 1–9*. 6th ed. Translated by Muhammad Muhsin Khan. Lahore: Kazi, 1983.

———. The Translation of the Meanings of Summarized Sahih al-Bukhari: Arabic-English. Edited by Ahmad ibn Ahmad Zabidi. Translated by Muhammad Muhsin Khan. Riyadh: Maktaba Dar us-Salam, 1997.

al-Tabari. *The History of al-tabari: Ta'rikh al-Rusl wa'l Muluk, Vol. 10, The Conquest of Arabia*. Albany, NY: State University of New York, 1985.

Avenanti, Sirigu, et al. "Racial Bias Reduces Empathic Sensorimotor Resonance with Other-Race Pain." *Current Biology* 20 (June 8, 2010) 1018–22. https://www.academia.edu/1031618/Avenanti_A_Sirigu_A_Aglioti_SM_2010_._Racial_bias_reduces_empathic_sensorimotor_resonance_with_other-race_pain._Current_Biology_20_1018-1022.

Benmelech, Efraim, and Esteban F. Klor. "What Explains the Flow of Foreign Fighters to ISIS?" NBER Working Paper, November 2016. https://scholars.huji.ac.il/eklor/publications/what-explains-flow-foreign-fighters-isis.

Bianchi, Robert R. *Guest of God: Pilgrimage and Politics in the Islamic World*. New York: Oxford University Press, 2004.

Bridge Initiative Team. "News Study Analyzes Media Coverage of Islam over Time." *Islamophobia Reframed* (website), April 24, 2015. http://bridge.georgetown.edu/new-study-analyzes-media-coverage-of-islam-over-time/.

Charles, Maria. "What Gender Is Science?" In *Contexts*, Spring 2011, 22–28. http://www.soc.ucsb.edu/faculty/mariacharles/documents/WhatGenderisScience.pdf.

"Checkpoints 101." *Occupied Palestine* (blog), accessed April 25, 2017. https://occupiedpalestine.wordpress.com/special-topics/checkpoints/.

Cook, David. *Understanding Jihad*. Berkeley, CA: University of California Press, 2015.

de Gruchy, John, with Steve de Gruchy. *The Church Struggle in South Africa*. London: SCM, 2004.

"Deep Ecumenism." Aleph: Alliance for Jewish Renewal. https://aleph.org/projects/deep-ecumenism.

"Denmark Virtual Jewish History Tour." Jewish Virtual Library. jewishvirtuallibrary.org/jsource/vjw/Denmark.html.

Edwards, Jonathan. "Sinners in the Hands of an Angry God." 1741.

Feldberg, Michael. "Rabbi Gittelsohn's Iwo Jima Sermon." *My Jewish Learning* (website). http://www.myjewishlearning.com/article/rabbi-gittelsohns-iwo-jima-sermon/.

Fenton, Siobhan. "Lahore Blast: Taliban Bomb Kills at Least 70 and Injures 300 Outside Public Park in Eastern Pakistan." *Independent*, March 27, 2016. http://www.independent.co.uk/news/world/asia/lahore-blast-15-killed-and-at-least-30-injured-outside-public-park-in-eastern-pakistan-a6955366.html.

Fetters, Ashley. "Chinua Achebe's Legacy, in His Own Words." *Atlantic*, March 22, 2013. https://www.theatlantic.com/entertainment/archive/2013/03/chinua-achebes-legacy-in-his-own-words/274297/.

Flannery, Edward H. *The Anguish of the Jews: A Catholic Priest Writes of 23 Centuries of Anti-Semitism*. New York: Macmillan, 1965.

Fleischner, Eva. *Auschwitz: Beginning of a New Era?* New York: KTAV, 1977.

Floyd, Chris. "War without End, Amen: The Reality of America's Aggression against Iraq." chris-floyd.com, December 16, 2011. http://www.chris-floyd.com/component/content/article/1-latest-news/2200-war-without-end-amen-the-reality-of-americas-aggression-against-iraq-.html.

Flusser, David. "Abraham and the Upanishads." *Immanuel: A Journal of Religious Thought and Research in Israel,* 20 (Spring 1986) 53–61. http://www.etrfi.info/immanuel/20/Immanuel_20_053.pdf.

Green, Arthur. *Radical Judaism: Rethinking God and Tradition*. New Haven, CT: Yale University Press, 2010.

Haldon, John. *The Palgrave Atlas of Byzantine History*. New York: Palgrave Macmillan, 2005.

Heschel, A. J. "Religion and Race." In *The Insecurity of Freedom*. Philadelphia: Jewish Publication Society, 1966.

Hirschhorn, Linda. "Sarah and Hagar." Linda Hirschhorn website, 1987. http://www.lindahirschhorn.com/cds/more_than_luck/sarah_and_hagar.html.

Hornsey, Matthew J. "Linking Superiority in the Interpersonal and Intergroup Domains." *Journal of Social Psychology* 143, no. 4 (August 2003) 479–91.

Human Relations and the South African Scene. A Dutch Reformed Church (*Nederduitse Gereformeerde Kerk*, NGK) synodical document, 1974. In *The Church Struggle in South Africa*. 25th anniversary edition, by John W. de Gruchy and Steve de Gruchy. Minneapolis, MN: Fortress, 2005.

ibn Anas, Malik. *Muwatta' Imam Malik*. Translated by Christopher Ward. Lahore: S. Muhammad Ashraf, 1980.

Jespersen, Knud J. V. *A History of Denmark*. 2d ed. Translated by Christopher Ward. New York: Palgrave Macmillan, 2011.

"John Lewis: Love in Action." *On Being with Krista Tippett*, transcript of interview, January 26, 2017. https://onbeing.org/programs/john-lewis-love-in-action/.

Kahf, Mohja. "All Good." In *Hagar Poems*, 33–35. Fayetteville, AR: University of Arkansas Press, 2016.

Kaplan, Edward. *Spiritual Radical: Abraham Joshua Heschel in America*. New Haven, CT: Yale University Press, 2007.

Katz, Claire. "The Voice of God and the Face of the Other." In *Journal of Textual Reasoning*. http://jtr.shanti.virginia.edu/volume-2-number-1/the-voice-of-god-and-the-face-of-the-other/.

Kentane, Bie. "The Children of Iraq: 'Was the Price Worth It?'" *Global Research*, May 7, 2012. http://www.globalresearch.ca/the-children-of-iraq-was-the-price-worth-it/30760.

Levine, A. J., and M. Z. Brettler. *Jewish Annotated New Testament*. New York: Oxford University Press, 2011.

"MI5 Report Challenges Views on Terrorism in Britain." *The Guardian*, August 20, 2008. https://www.theguardian.com/uk/2008/aug/20/uksecurity.terrorism1.

Milosz, Czeslaw. "Learning." In *Road-side Dog*, 60. New York: Farrar, Straus and Giroux, 1998.

———. "Report." In *Facing the River: New Poems*, 13–15. Hopewell, NJ: Ecco, 1995.

Morinis, Alan. "Through a Mussar Lens." *Yashar: Newsletter of The Mussar Institute*, January 2017. http://mussarinstitute.org/Yashar/2017-01/mussar_lens.php.

"Muslim Women: Past and Present." Women's Islamic Initiative in Spirituality and Equality (WISE). http://www.wisemuslimwomen.org/muslimwomen/summary/C254/category-search/100_extraordinary_muslim_women.

Naidoo, Beverly. "Frequently Asked Questions." Beverley Naidoo website. www.beverleynaidoo.com/faqs.htm.

"Names of Righteous by Country." Yad Vashem. January 1, 2017. http://www.yadvashem.org/righteous/statistics.

"A New Generation Expresses its Skepticism and Frustration with Christianity." *Barna: Update*, September 21, 2007. https://www.barna.com/research/a-new-generation-expresses-its-skepticism-and-frustration-with-christianity/.

"Nicholas V, Papal Bulls of," in *The Historical Encyclopedia of World Slavery*," vol. 2, edited by Junius P. Rodriguez, 469. Santa Barbara, CA: ABC-CLIO, 1997.

Nye, Naomi Shihab. "To Any Would-Be Terrorists." Islamic Studies, Islam, Arabic, and Religion website of Dr. Alan Godlas, University of Georgia, February 1, 2001. http://islam.uga.edu/shihabnye.html.

Ojiaku, Princess. "Is Everybody a Racist?" *Aeon*, March 21, 2016. https://aeon.co/essays/unconscious-racism-is-pervasive-starts-early-and-can-be-deadly.

Philadelphia Interfaith Walk for Peace and Reconciliation. http://www.interfaithpeacewalk.org/.

Project Implicit. 2011. https://implicit.harvard.edu/implicit/.

Putnam, Robert D. *Our Kids: The American Dream in Crisis*. New York: Simon and Schuster, 2015.

Rice, Zak Cheney. "There's a Massive Double Standard in the Global Response to Sunday's Bombing in Ankara." *Mic*, March 14, 2016. https://mic.com/articles/137848/massive-double-standard-in-global-response-to-ankara-bombing-exposed-in-this-facebook-post#.mt1dm30AV.

Rios, Edwin, and Dave Gilson. "11 Charts that Show Income Inequality Isn't Getting Better Anytime Soon." *Mother Jones*, December 22, 2016. http://www.motherjones.com/politics/2016/12/america-income-inequality-wealth-net-worth-charts.

Sacks, Jonathan. *The Dignity of Difference: How to Avoid the Clash of Civilizations*. London: Continuum, 2002.

Salim, Mustafa, and Liz Sly. "Islamic State Suicide Bomber Kills Dozens at a Stadium South of Baghdad." *Washington Post*, March 26, 2016. https://www.washingtonpost.com/world/middle_east/suicide-bomber-kills-at-least-25-at-a-soccer-stadium-south-of-baghdad/2016/03/25/36a2971c-f2b2-11e5-a2a3-d4e9697917d1_story.html.

Schaeffer, Frank. "How I (and Other 'Pro-Life' Leaders) Contributed to Dr. Tiller's Murder." *Huffington Post*, July 2, 2009. www.huffingtonpost.com/frank-schaeffer/how-i-and-other-pro-life_b_209747.html.

Schanzer, Kurzman, et al. *Anti-Terror Lessons of Muslim-Americans*. Duke University Faculty Database System, January 6, 2010. https://fds.duke.edu/db/attachment/1255.

Schwartz, Regina. *The Curse of Cain: The Violent Legacy of Monotheism*. Chicago: University of Chicago, 1997.

Shaharudi, Nur al-Din. *al-Maraja 'iyah al-Diniya wa Maraja' al-Imamiya*. Tahran: al-Mu 'allif, 1995

Sisterhood of Salaam Shalom. https://sosspeace.org/.

"The Smell Report." Social Issues Research Center (website). http://www.sirc.org/publik/smell_culture.html.

Soloveitchik, Joseph. *Abraham's Journey: Reflections on the Life of the Founding Patriarch*. New York: KTAV, 2008.

Stone, Ira. *A Responsible Life: The Spiritual Path of Mussar*. New York: Aviv, 2006.

Washington's Blog. "Non-Muslims Carried Out More than 90% of All Terrorist Attacks in America." *Global Research*, May 1, 2013. http://www.globalresearch.ca/non-muslims-carried-out-more-than-90-of-all-terrorist-attacks-in-america/5333619.

"We Don't Want You Here." The PCFF, July 17, 2014. https://www.youtube.com/watch?v=rmepq3WpyMM.

Werner, Emmy E. *A Conspiracy of Decency: The Rescue of the Danish Jews During World War II*. Cambridge, MA: Westview, 2002.

Wilson, Lydia. "What I Discovered from Interviewing Imprisoned ISIS Fighters." In *The Nation*, October 21, 2015. https://www.thenation.com/article/what-i-discovered-from-interviewing-isis-prisoners/.

Yahil, Leni. *The Rescue of Danish Jewry: Test of a Democracy*. Philadelphia: Jewish Publication Society of America, 1969.

"Yemen Suicide Bomb Attacks Kill 26 in Aden." *ABC News*, March 25, 2016. http://www.abc.net.au/news/2016-03-26/suicide-bombings-hit-yemen/7277452.